# *Parenting Generation Screen* Endorsem



This is *the* book for helping parents create a me
you lead your kids toward making good decisio
opinion, Jonathan McKee is one of the leading experts in the world of guiding our kids through this important part of their life. This will be my go-to book.

**JIM BURNS, PHD,** president of HomeWord; author of *The Purity Code* and *Understanding Your Teen*

I think I will keep a stack of Jonathan's *Parenting Generation Screen* in my car to hand to parents I dialogue with each week . . . because it deals with the exact issues they ask me about: When do I give my kids a phone? Should I let them have it in their bedroom? How much social media is too much? I love the wisdom and practicality Jonathan brings to his books . . . and wish I had this one five to ten years ago!

**SHAUNTI FELDHAHN,** bestselling author of *For Women Only* and *For Parents Only*

*Parenting Generation Screen* is the book I have been waiting for. As a parent of high school, junior high, and elementary students, it helped me tremendously to think through reasonable technological boundaries with my kids. I appreciate that Jonathan offers some practical, research-based suggestions, yet he focuses on the importance of relationships. Every parent needs to read this book and discuss it with others.

**SEAN MCDOWELL, PHD,** associate professor of apologetics at Talbot School of Theology; author of *Chasing Love: Sex, Love and Relationships in a Confused Culture*

If your kid is about to graduate grade school or high school—or is anywhere in between—then you need Jonathan McKee's *Parenting Generation Screen.* McKee jams practical wisdom on every page and even offers discussion questions at the end of each chapter that will jumpstart conversations between you and your teens. Get this book—and get your kid back!

**DAVID R. SMITH,** author of *Christianity . . . It's Like This: An Uncomplicated Look at What It Means to Be a Christ-Follower*

In a world where the average age that kids get their first smartphone is just ten years old, parents are struggling to keep up with their children's interaction with screens. *Parenting Generation Screen* gives moms and dads the tools they need not only to provide healthy screen limits but also to engage their kids in ongoing conversations about becoming screen-wise.

**DOUG FIELDS,** author of *Intentional Parenting*

No generation of young people has ever been so impacted by technology. It may be years before we understand the true impact of screen devices on our kids. In the meantime, Jonathan McKee—my go-to youth expert—has written a powerful and concise primer to help you navigate the world of screens. *Parenting Generation Screen* will help you engage your kids, understand their challenges, and set proper boundaries. If you've got young people in your life, *Parenting Generation Screen* is yet another essential resource from Jonathan McKee.

**J. WARNER WALLACE,** detective featured on *Dateline*; author of *So the Next Generation Will Know: Preparing Young Christians for a Challenging World*

I'm so thankful that Jonathan wrote this book! It's a literal guide to navigating cultural differences created by screens. Not only is it a great resource for parents, but I would especially encourage grandparents to read it as well.

**GREG ALDERMAN,** senior pastor of Christ Community Church, California

As a parent, we can often feel uninformed and overwhelmed when it comes to the world of smart phones and social media. Jonathan has given us yet another valuable resource, weaving compelling information with practical action steps and biblical wisdom. This is the handbook parents have been searching for to provide help navigating the challenges of parenting Generation Screen.

**ROB CHAGDES,** family ministry pastor of Prairie Lakes Church, Iowa

The content of the book will equip and guide you as parents in a digital world. I believe that Jonathan's book needs to be in every parent's hand as it will make you thrive in helping your kids make wise decisions.

**ANDREW MCCOURT,** senior pastor of Bayside Church

Improper use of screens is the most serious threat to our kids' emotional, intellectual, and physical health in this decade. Every parent knows that screens can be devastating for kids but has no idea how to set boundaries that kids will actually honor. We are afraid. In *Parenting Generation Screen*, Jonathan gives advice that not only dissipates that fear but teaches us step by step how to set those boundaries. Most extraordinary is that his method actually helps kids grow closer to their parents. No parent in the 21st century can afford not to read this book.

**MEG MEEKER, MD,** national bestselling author of *Strong Fathers, Strong Daughters*; find her at: meekerparenting.com

Jonathan McKee offers a gift all 21st-century parents need—practical tips of what to say and do that convert technology from a barrier that keeps families apart to a bridge that draws us closer together.

**KARA POWELL, PHD,** executive director of the Fuller Youth Institute; chief of leadership formation at Fuller Seminary; co-author of *3 Big Questions That Change Every Teenager*

If there was such a thing as an adolescence survival kit for parents, this book would be in it. The wisdom here goes well beyond dealing with teens and screens and speaks to the hearts of parents and parenting. Read this book and you'll not only be prepared for the road ahead, but you'll also have a stronger relationship with your kids.

**PETE SUTTON,** pastor of student ministry at The Compass Church

Jonathan McKee has become a trusted voice for parents and teens striving to navigate 21st-century culture in wise and discerning ways. In his latest book, he examines screen use and identifies ways families can avoid technology's biggest stumbling blocks. This is a comprehensive, must-read handbook for any parent whose kids have screens in their hands.

**JIM DALY,** president of Focus on the Family

While there is much to be said about screens and the impact these new frontiers have on our teens, I am even more appreciative of this tool that Jonathan McKee is putting in the hands of parents. He reminds us all that conversations and relationships are better than rules and that parents can still have the greatest influence in the lives of their teens. Don't rush through this book and don't react; but after things sink in, I encourage you to act. Even though limiting screen time matters, communicating with your teen about it matters more.

**JONATHAN MEYER,** founder of Ignite Youth Leadership Conference; veteran youth pastor of 25+ years

Wow—every parent needs this book! Not only will it answer a multitude of questions you have, but it will help you ask and answer questions you have never even thought about. Jonathan's book is the most practical and comprehensive book I've ever read on this topic. Once you read it, you'll want to give it to every parent you know.

> **CYNTHIA ULRICH TOBIAS,** bestselling author of 14 books, including *You Can't Make Me (But I Can Be Persuaded)*, *The Way They Learn*, *The Way We Work*, *Every Child Can Succeed*, and *A Woman of Strength and Purpose*

Read this easy-to-read-and-learn-from book now. Jonathan's insights will encourage both your heart and your mind. His compassion for parents and children of all ages comes through on every page. He won't shame you, and you'll feel no guilt—no matter what you have or haven't done. His ideas are important, founded on solid research and many relevant experiences, and absolutely achievable. Best of all, he shows you how to involve your children in planning to be more screen-wise. You and they will know what to do, when to do it, how to do it, and why to do it. You will all have plenty of hope for the future!

> **DR. KATHY KOCH,** founder of Celebrate Kids, Inc.; author of *Screens and Teens*, *8 Great Smarts*, *Start with the Heart*, and *Five to Thrive*

Practical. Concrete. Relational. Realistic. Jonathan McKee's new book *Parenting Generation Screen: Guiding Your Kids to Be Wise in a Digital World* delivers winsome wisdom for parents grappling with the omnipresent issue of tweens and teens, screens and social media. If you feel like you've already made big mistakes or if your kids are on the cusp of the getting their first phone, Jonathan McKee's insights from years of ministering to parents will offer you and your family guidance and hope.

> **ADAM R. HOLZ,** director of Focus on the Family's entertainment and technology website *Plugged In*

We are in the midst of a digital revolution that is fundamentally changing our world, and our children are at the frontlines. As a pastor and father, I desperately need help navigating this unknown, ever-changing digital landscape. Jonathan's ability to see through the eyes of young people while simultaneously being able to see beyond this perspective as a parent and youth ministry expert makes him the near perfect guide for navigating the challenges of parenting Generation Screen. His practical, relationship-oriented, and well-researched approach has helped me invite my family and my congregation into crucial conversations about how we might become screen-wise. I want to get this book into the hands of every parent in my congregation.

**PAUL ANDERSON,** lead pastor of Grace Valley Fellowship

I realize that you expect an endorsement to say "this book is great, you should read it . . ."; but I'm telling you if you have a kid who likes their phone, this book is fantastic, and I'd beg you to read it! Not only does Jonathan give you insider info on things that so many parents aren't aware of, but he gives super-practical ideas for navigating phone-life. He's not just some distant "expert"; he's an experienced dad who has counseled parents nationwide. You already know that parenting is not for the faint of heart . . . but I believe this book can give your heart more courage and wisdom—and help your kids win!

**SCOTT RUBIN,** next generation director of EastSide Christian Church

You don't have to parent Generation Screen out of fear, frustration, or a lack of knowledge anymore. Years of working with teenagers (and raising his own kids) have made Jonathan McKee a voice of reason and source of wisdom. Instead of rationalizing the warning signs of too much screen time, you'll be inspired to engage with your child with renewed purpose. There's too much at stake to let screens take over your child's life. It's time to truly connect again face to face in families, and this book will help you do that.

**ARLENE PELLICANE,** author of *Parents Rising* and co-author of *Screen Kids* (with Dr. Gary Chapman)

Parenting teenagers is the single hardest thing I've ever done in my life. Any parent who doesn't agree isn't doing it right, and almost no parent alive would say that screens and smartphones (and everything those include) make it easier. We need help! That's what Jonathan offers—practical, humble, honest, and rooted-in-excellence parenting principles that supersede the details.

**MARK OESTREICHER,** founder and partner of The Youth Cartel; author of *Understanding Your Young Teen, A Parent's Guide to Understanding Teenage Brains* and other books.

The title of this book could be: *Everything I Need to Know about Setting Limits on Screens AND Building a Relationship with My Children.* Seriously, I haven't read a more practical, easy-to-read guide on helping parents understand everything they need to know about kids and screens and still manage the relationship in a respectful, not controlling manner. This guide answers every question you've ever asked about screen time and gives you the tools for building trust in your kids as you help them learn how to be responsible. Every parent needs to read this book before buying their child a phone.

**JOSHUA STRAUB, PHD,** cofounder and president of Famous at Home

Every parent needs this insightful, easy-to-use guidebook to navigate the confusing and sometimes dangerous digital world of screens. Jonathan McKee is a trusted source for parents, and in *Parenting Generation Screen: Guiding Your Kids to Be Wise in a Digital World*, he shines in his element. Utilizing the latest research and years of experience, he weaves thoughtful parenting advice, how-to blueprints for those difficult conversations, and hope-filled wisdom, giving you success in setting boundaries while teaching the "why" without damaging relationships. Here are some of the many wisdom threads woven throughout this book: Limits don't work without love; boundaries are meaningless without bonding; correction is ineffective without connection. Jonathan utilizes these principles masterfully throughout the book to help you keep the main thing the main thing: strengthening your relationships with your kids as you guide them through the digital maze. This book is a must for your parenting toolbelt!

**CARRIE ABBOTT,** president of The Legacy Institute; host of *Relationship Insights* radio and podcast

Once again, Jonathan McKee delivers a helpful resource for parents. *Parenting Generation Screen* is must-read for parents as they navigate the uncertain waters of smart phones and teens. It's a 21st-century conundrum of screens and social media and the ill-equipped kids who have them. Herein this book lies a ton of wisdom for parents—enabling them to take a well-thought-out approach to this issue that must be faced.

**BOB JOHNS,** youth pastor at First Woodway Baptist Church

# Parenting Generation Screen

Guiding Your
Kids to Be
Wise in a
Digital World

# Parenting
# Generation
# Screen

## Jonathan McKee

FOCUS
ON THE FAMILY.

A Focus on the Family Resource
Published by Tyndale House Publishers
Carol Stream, Illinois

# Contents

## CHAPTER 1

# They Don't Tell You This Stuff

*Everything you wish you'd known
before you bought your kids their first screen*

"DAD, CAN I HAVE THE KEYS TO THE SUV?"

This question doesn't sound unusual—unless it comes from your ten-year-old.

Picture it. Your daughter walks into the room and says, "Dad, I'd like the keys so I can drive over to pick up my friends and then go meet a bunch of guys we've never met before and see what happens."

How would you respond?

The answer is pretty clear. I don't know a parent who would give their ten-year-old this kind of freedom.

But the majority of parents do . . . *when they give their child a phone.*

## Good Intentions

Don't feel bad if you've already handed your kid a smartphone. Most moms and dads didn't have a clue about the dangers when they did that.

In fact, most parents I meet at my parenting workshops tell me that the whole reason they gave smartphones to their kids was to keep them safe.

"I just wanted them to be able to call me in case of an emergency."

"This way I can connect with them at all times."

"My kids are in sports and need to call me for a ride home."

I honestly think these parents' intentions were pure. They just had no idea that they were "throwing the keys" to their ten-year-old.

I'm using this example intentionally because ten is the average age a kid gets a phone in this country. In fact, the number of kids who have smartphones only increases with age:

- 53 percent of eleven-year-olds
- 69 percent of twelve-year-olds
- 72 percent of thirteen-year-olds[1]

Those numbers represent the kids *who aren't even in high school yet.*

By high school, the overwhelming majority of teens are "connected." Eighty-nine percent of teenagers (ages thirteen to seventeen) have smartphones,[2] and 95 percent have access to the most popular social media platforms.[3]

The kids who *don't* have devices feel a little out of place, and other kids tease them. "What do you mean you don't have a phone? Are you kidding? What are you, Amish or something? Hey, everyone, check it out. Braden's mommy doesn't let him have a phone!"

So for whatever reason, most of us have given our kids a device with potential far beyond what we ever would have predicted.

Like the mom of a kid I'll call Christine. This mom approached me at one of my parenting workshops after everyone else had left. I'd seen her standing off in the distance, noticeably anxious.

"Can I ask you a question?" she asked.

"Sure."

"It's about my daughter, Christine."

"How old is she?" I asked.

"Thirteen. And she currently isn't allowed to use her phone. I've taken it away."

"When did she first get a phone?"

"A year ago. But I told her no social media or any of that bad stuff."

"How'd that work out?"

"It didn't," she answered candidly. "She downloaded some social media app I didn't even know about."

"Did you have any parental controls set on her phone?"

She hung her head. "No. I didn't know how to do that."

"I totally understand," I offered in an attempt to comfort her. "It's hard to keep up today. So what happened?"

"She met some guy who told her everything she wanted to hear, and she'd talk with him until all hours of the night."

"How old did the guy *claim* he was?" (Keyword: *claim*.)

"Seventeen," she answered. "He said he went to our local high school. She's homeschooled."

Finishing her story for her, I said, "But you found out he wasn't a teenager at all, right?"

"Yeah." She looked at me with the "How did you know?" expression I usually see at my parenting workshops.

"So did he ask for a nude?" Again, I noticed the "How did you know?" look. "I ask because this happens all the time," I explained. "You're not alone. I've heard stories like yours from moms all over the country."

"Yes," she replied, answering my question about the nude photo. "He did."

"And did she send him a pic?"

The mom looked down. "Yes. Her"—she struggled for words—"her top."

"And everything changed once she sent the pic, right?"

"Yes. He started insisting they meet, or else he would show the photo to everyone."

"So did she meet up with him?"

"She set up a time, but then she told her friend, who told her mom, who in turn told me. We called the police. They're still trying to find him." She wiped away a single tear trickling down her cheek. "They don't tell you this stuff when you buy your kid a phone."

"No, they certainly don't."

The next week, another mom approached me after one of my workshops on the opposite side of the country.

"So how can I get my son to stop playing video games literally all day?" she asked.

"How long does he typically play?" I probed.

"During the school year, he plays from the time he gets home until late at night. Homework is an afterthought. In the summer, it's even worse. He wakes up at noon and picks up his controller before his feet hit the floor. If we don't call him down for dinner, he won't leave his room at all until he quits playing after midnight."

"Have you tried limiting his game time?" I asked.

"Yeah. But we found that he just sneaks it in when we're at work or at his sister's gymnastics. We've tried to take him with us, but he just complains and makes us all miserable. I hate to admit it, but it's just easier to let him stay in his room and play his stupid games."

And then she said it.

"I wish I'd known this before I bought him that stupid game system."

A few weeks later, twelve hundred miles away, another mom pulled me aside and asked, "How do I convince my daughter that her grades still matter, even if she wants to be a social media influencer?"

"What platform does she use?" I asked. "YouTube? TikTok?"

"YouTube. She posts a weekly vlog and has about nine hundred followers. She read an article somewhere that you only need five hundred to be an influencer. She's scrapped her plans to become a teacher and wants to be a full-time influencer now. She won't even look at college applications."

"You're not alone," I assured the mom. "Eighty-six percent of young people want to be an influencer of some sort today.[4] But less than one-twentieth of one percent are able to do it full-time."

Then she said it.

"The school didn't tell me this stuff when they issued her a laptop for distance learning."

A month later, in my home state, a dad asked me, "What do you do when you discover your son looking at inappropriate pictures in his room late at night?"

"Does he always have his phone in his bedroom?" I asked.

"Not now. But when I took it away, I caught him again, this time with an old phone that wasn't even activated. We didn't remember he still had that phone."

"Yeah, old phones or tablets can still connect to Wi-Fi even if they don't have an active data plan. I constantly hear parents telling me stories of kids using old devices in their bedrooms."

And then I heard it again: "How come no one tells you this stuff?"

That's exactly why I wrote this book.

## A Tap Away

It's true. No one tells you this stuff when you're buying your kids their first screens for Christmas. And kids aren't required to learn anything about becoming screenwise before they get a device. Most parents just throw their kids the keys.

Sadly, the examples I just shared aren't unique. I'm being completely honest when I tell you I hear stories like these in *every* city where I speak, and not just from parents. In fact, whenever I speak about this at school assemblies, kids will come up to me afterward and ask questions about something that just happened at their school . . . on their device . . . that Mom and Dad didn't know about . . . that's causing an unprecedented amount of anxiety, depression, and tears.

That's just it. It's not that screens are bad, but they've unarguably exposed kids to greater risks to their physical safety and mental health. And even though many of us experienced similar risks when we were young, our modern devices have only amplified the risks for two simple reasons:

- They've increased accessibility to harmful content and dangerous people.
- They've decreased accountability.

Porn was available when I was a teenager, but kids had to actually make an effort to find it. Today, it's just a tap away, with the devices we all carry in our pockets. Pedophiles have existed for millennia, but now they have unrestricted access to kids who are sharing way too much about themselves and are desperate for "followers." Young people have always struggled with self-esteem, but now they carry devices with them that tell them exactly how many more friends other people have, how many more followers others have, and precisely how they measure up to everyone else who is more popular, better looking, and more creative than they are. And these devices follow our kids literally everywhere: school, home, the bedroom, the bathroom . . .

*Increased accessibility; decreased accountability.*

> *Porn was available when I was a teenager, but kids had to actually make an effort to find it. Today, it's just a tap away.*

It's no wonder many mental-health experts, like Dr. Jean Twenge, claim that smartphones may be destroying a generation of teens.[5]

But it doesn't have to be this way.

## It's Not Too Late

Parents *can* do something to protect their children. And no, the answer isn't banning your kids from screens until they're adults and out of the house. Far from it.

But at the same time, you don't need to "throw the keys" to your ten-year-old.

Consider Christine for just a moment—the true story I shared earlier about a thirteen-year-old girl whose mom ended up taking away her phone. If Christine's mom had a do-over, I know she would rethink her parenting decisions and would probably handle the following issues differently:

1. Christine's mom chose to give Christine a phone at the age of twelve, while most experts advise parents to wait until their kids are older and a little more mature. (We'll cover this in detail in chapter 3.) Christine's mom didn't know this. In fact, Christine was one of the last kids in her church youth group to get a phone. The pressure was on. So her mom finally caved and bought her a phone. *She threw her twelve-year-old the keys.*

2. Christine's mom told Christine, "No social media or any of that bad stuff," but she never enforced the rule. So it wasn't long before Christine cheated and got on social media. A lot of parents allow young kids to use social media, such as Snapchat, Instagram, TikTok, and Twitter, but are unaware that kids under thirteen can't even download those apps without lying about their age. (More on that in chapter 3.) Kids under thirteen shouldn't be on social media, period. At least Christine's mom said no to social media, but . . .

3. She didn't set any parental controls. Christine was free to do whatever she wanted with her device. Imagine if her device were a car. She'd be free to drive as fast as she wanted, seat belt off, radio blasting, friends hanging out the sunroof—with no cops patrolling the roads. (We'll talk more about helpful parental controls in chapter 8.)

4. She didn't set limits. Christine's mom said that Christine was talking with this guy "until all hours of the night." That's a lot of hours. We live in a world where teens average nine hours and forty-nine minutes a day soaking in entertainment media, including seven hours and twenty-two minutes of screen media.[6] But almost every expert out there recommends that parents limit screen time to some degree, especially social media. Yes, there has been a lot of debate about this topic, with overreactions on both sides, but you'll discover that almost all experts agree on a few undebatable guidelines about screen time—including the point that endless access to social media throughout the night should definitely not be allowed. (More on screen time in chapter 6.)

5. She allowed Christine to have the phone in her bedroom at night. Christine wasn't just clocking the hours on her phone; she was clocking "after hours" when she was supposed to be sleeping. That means she was one of 79 percent of young people who keep their phones in their bedrooms every night,[7] even though every mental-health professional would say this is a very bad idea. (We'll talk more about the effects of allowing phones in the bedroom in chapter 4.)

6. Christine's mom never told her daughter what predatory behaviors look like. So Christine wasn't suspicious when a stranger direct-messaged (DM'ed) her, asking all the right questions while

avoiding FaceTime or other platforms where she could see him in real time. She wasn't even alarmed when he asked her to send a "nude" and eventually meet in person. This guy was following the predator's handbook word for word, but Christine didn't know how to recognize predatory behaviors. (We'll talk about these in detail in chapter 7.)

7. Christine had no idea any of these things would happen, because her mom never talked with her about them. Even if her mom had set every boundary and parental control available (remember that Christine was a very sheltered homeschool kid), the decision about how to use social media was ultimately Christine's. *Rules won't raise your kids.* You actually need to teach them discernment so they can make decisions on their own. (We'll flesh this out throughout the book.)

> *Rules won't raise your kids.*
> *You actually need to teach them discernment so they can make decisions on their own.*

It's not too late for Christine and her mom. The two of them are starting over. Christine's mom is waiting a while before returning her phone. In fact, they're now meeting for breakfast once a week, reading my book *The Teen's Guide to Social Media and Mobile Devices* together, and talking about real-world issues, including what Christine is posting, whom she's friending, and what she's streaming. Christine's mom is balancing boundaries and bonding. She's not just enforcing rules; she's also being proactive by engaging Christine in meaningful conversations about stuff that matters.

If you're a parent (or guardian) who wants to be proactive about social media use, you've probably asked yourself these questions:

- At what age should I give my kids a phone, or any other device for that matter? After all, their friends already have phones.

- What if I've already given my kids a phone? What now? Do I take their phones away until they're older?

- Should I set parental controls? And if so, which ones? Should these controls change as my kids get older?

- At what age should I allow my kids on social media? What effect does social media actually have on their mental health? Is it even safe?

- What about screen time? Does it really affect kids? How many hours are too many? Does the number of hours change on the weekends, during the summer, or when our country quarantines everyone in their homes with nothing to do?

- What if my kids want to take their devices into their bedrooms at night? The overwhelming majority of kids do, so are my kids going to be the class oddballs if I require them to give me their phones every night?

- How do I guard my kids from online predators? Young people all want more followers today, so they "friend" anyone and everyone. What are the ramifications of this, and how can I help my kids recognize predatory behaviors?

- Most importantly, how am I supposed to help my kids with all of this when they seem to know more about technology than I do? How can I teach discernment with a device I don't even understand?

Good questions. Let me comfort you right away by letting you know that it's almost impossible to keep up with technology . . . *and you don't need to.* You don't need to be an expert on every new app released and every musical artist your kids encounter. You only need to understand some broad safety principles that apply to all devices, apps, and entertainment and then exercise discernment.

If you have this basic understanding, when your kid asks you some random question, such as "Mom, Dad . . . can I download the app Houseparty?" you'll be able to answer, "I don't know. But let's check it out together."

And you'll know exactly what to check for.

So let's dive in. The best way to begin is by connecting before correcting.

## Discussion Questions

1. Be honest: what's your favorite screen device and why?

2. What are your kids' favorite screen devices and screen activities?

3. Why do you think parents are giving their kids devices at increasingly younger ages, without providing any guidance as to how to be wise with their screens?

4. How have you noticed the increased accessibility to harmful content via screens decreasing young people's accountability regarding the kinds of entertainment they're streaming?

5. Jonathan cited seven issues that Christine's mom would probably rethink and handle differently if she had a do-over. Name just one of these issues that stood out to you as vitally important.

6. Jonathan said, "Rules won't raise your kids. You actually need to teach them discernment so they can make decisions on their own." What is one way you could try this with your kids this week?

## CHAPTER 2

# Connection before Correction

*How to replace overreaction with interaction*

I MET MY WIFE, LORI, when I was nineteen years old, fell madly in love with her, and married her at twenty. The only problem?

I was just a stupid kid.

I didn't know how to get along with someone 24/7. That's, like, full-time!

So the first few years of our marriage were the relational school of hard knocks for me. I learned almost everything by trial and error. For example, when Lori came home tired from work, ranting about her day, and asked questions like "What am I supposed to do?" it took me a few years to realize that she didn't actually want an answer.

That was a tough lesson to learn. After all, I'm a fixer. Whenever Lori shared her work frustrations, I was quick to offer my theories for how to fix the situation.

But she didn't want me to fix her problems. She just wanted me to listen.

Many of you might also be fixers. Some of you don't even feel the need to let others finish their thoughts. You interrupt, saying, "I know what you're going to say, and here's what you should do . . . "

Lori didn't want me to tell her what to do. She simply wanted me to understand and reply, "That stinks. You sound frustrated. I would be irritated too. Let's go eat mounds of ice cream."

Lori wanted empathy (and Ben & Jerry's Chunky Monkey), not a quick fix from me.

Don't we all?

## Resist the Quick Fix

That's the thing about our kids and their screens: quick fixes won't work. When many of us read a book like this or attend a parenting workshop that warns us of social media risks and/or recommends certain screen limits, our first reaction is to impose a quick fix.

A speaker shares a few examples, and we feel compelled to go home and lay down the law with our kids. Or instead of reading the whole book, some of us read half a chapter and call a family meeting.

"Kids. Downstairs. Now! And bring your phones."

(Be honest: You were already thinking about doing this, weren't you?)

Hold off for a few days. Maybe even a couple of weeks. Resist the urge to impose a quick fix, overreacting and confiscating your kids' screens.

*I'm not suggesting you let your kids do whatever they want. I'm just recommending you put connection before correction.*

In the 2020 report *Tweens, Teens, Tech, and Mental Health*, researchers said, "Conflict over screens is common in families and, in many cases, this conflict is likely to be more harmful to adolescents' mental health than screen time itself."[1]

Don't worry. I'm not suggesting you let your kids do whatever they want. I'm just recommending you put connection *before* correction.

Why?

Because the old adage is true: *rules without relationship only lead to rebellion.* I've seen it happen hundreds of times. Moms and dads want to raise their kids right, so they simply roll out the rules, followed with "Because I said so."

But here's the thing:

- Limits don't work without love.
- Boundaries are meaningless without bonding.
- Correction is ineffective without connection.

I find it interesting that the most fundamental parenting passage in the Bible doesn't recommend that we just set parental controls on our kids' devices and walk away. Take a peek at Deuteronomy 6:6-7 (NIV):

> These commandments that I give you today are to be on your hearts. Impress them on your children. Talk about them when you sit at home and when you walk along the road, when you lie down and when you get up.

These verses recommend doing much more than setting parental controls or porn blockers. Do you want to actually pass on values to your kids? Here's how: talk about them when you're sitting together at home, when you're walking along the road, when you're lying down, and when you're getting up.

Talk.

In the morning, during the day, at night.

That's a pretty clear picture of what dialogue looks like. Engaging your kids in conversation while you're driving to school in the morning, running to the store together, sitting around the dinner table, or tucking them into bed at night. This is Connection 101. These conversations pave the way to understanding your family values—the why behind any necessary rules or correction.

It's connection before correction.

Besides, connection is a far more effective teaching tool than correction.

That's important. Read that again.

*Connection is a far more effective teaching tool than correction.*

Again, I'm *not* saying don't correct your kids. I'm not one of those parents who think they should let their kids do whatever they want. Far from it. This book is full of helpful guardrails that can save your kids a lotta grief (and *a lotta* is a lot). But here's the reality of the situation: Your kids will learn values from you far better through times of connection than from the rules you impose.

> **Your kids will learn values from you far better through times of connection than from the rules you impose.**

Your kids absorbed *far more* truth from you that night you hung out with them talking by the campfire than when you installed porn filters on their computer.

I'm not saying don't have porn filters. I'm just saying that porn filters without conversations about God's design for sex and intimacy are weak.

Connection before correction.

So press the Pause button on laying down the law for the moment. By that I mean resist the urge to take screens away or impose new rules while you're in the middle of this book.

As you're reading this book over the next few weeks, don't

- confiscate screens,
- express regret for giving your kids screens in the first place,
- rant about the negatives of social media, or
- impose new screen limits.

Hold off on correction. Press the Pause button to avoid overreacting. Let's replace overreaction with interaction. You're going to have plenty of time for correction . . . after you focus on connection.

So how can you proactively place connection before correction? What does that actually look like?

Glad you asked. It took me a while to figure out, but I learned by trial and error. The following five steps helped me tremendously and have helped thousands of parents who have attended my workshops. We'll come back to these steps again and again throughout the book as we talk about helping your kids learn the important principle of becoming screenwise.

## Five Steps to Placing Connection before Correction

### 1. Set Up a Family Meeting . . . but Don't Call It That

After almost thirty years of youth ministry, one of the most frequent complaints I've heard from kids is, "My parents don't understand."

And many don't.

Understanding begins with noticing and listening. Our kids have a deep desire to be noticed and heard. Sadly, when we're so buried in our own screens that we're oblivious to our kids, they will often retreat to their screens in search of someone who will notice them.

Let that reality sink in for a moment.

Little Jennifer isn't getting much attention from Daddy, so she flees to Instagram and TikTok to get male attention.

It doesn't have to be like this.

Give your kids a chance to be heard. One of the best ways to do this is through proactive connection. No, it doesn't need to be an "official" family meeting. It can be as simple as initiating a conversation with your kids after dinner.

For example, you could say, "Hey, everyone, before we leave the table tonight, I have just one question, and I'd love to hear from every one of you. That question is, 'If you had three hundred dollars to spend at Target, what would you buy and why?'"

Yes, I start every family meeting with a fun question. Our go-to question was always, "What were your high and low today?"

I start with a fun question for two reasons:

- First, it breaks the ice with a nonthreatening question kids can't possibly answer wrong. It's a safe question.

- Second, it creates a fun climate where everyone feels noticed and heard. Everybody gets a turn.

Once everyone finishes their turn, you can bring up the topic of discussion.

## 2. Ask Your Kids' Opinions

*Whatever topic of discussion you bring up, be sure to solicit your kids' opinons.* Resist the long lectures. Just state the topic or issue and immediately give everyone a chance to chime in uninterrupted.

Let's say you decide to tackle the subject of screen limits in your home. First, explain the situation, then ask your kids what they think. For example:

> I've noticed that a lot of us are retreating to our rooms for hours at a time, and we barely even see each other. Sometimes Mom

and I have even retreated to our own screens. Now, we all love our screens, but I'm just wondering, when does this become unhealthy? How much is too much? What do you think?

After posing the questions, give everyone a turn to answer and listen carefully to each of their responses.

This might sound basic, but listening can be quite hard for some parents. Especially if you're a fixer. Your tendency might be to interrupt and solve the problem right then and there.

Resist the urge to fix. Resist the urge to correct your kids in any way.

### 3. Practice Empathy

Instead, use these times of listening to practice empathy. Are you a good listener? Instead of just hearing what your kids say, do you put yourself in their shoes?

That's a pretty good metaphor for empathy—*putting yourself in someone else's shoes.* The goal of listening isn't just hearing or even understanding; it's much more than that. It's diving into your kids' worlds and trying to walk where they walk, to see life from their perspectives, to understand their viewpoints and maybe even feel what they're feeling.

Let's say your twelve-year-old daughter tells you she wants the social media app TikTok. Your first response might be to immediately shut her down. After all . . .

- Kids must be thirteen to sign up. If they aren't, they have to lie about their age to use the app. Your daughter is twelve. Case closed.

- The app doesn't filter out raunchy talk or language. It's hard to spend a few minutes on TikTok without hearing profane stuff.

- At the moment, the privacy setting for the app defaults to "public." You have to actually flip a switch to change the setting to "private" so you gain control to approve who follows you, views your videos, and comments on or "likes" your posts. But kids today don't want to change the default setting to private because this means fewer followers, and they're all about the followers. (More on this later in the book.)

So when your daughter says she wants to sign up for TikTok, your first impulse may be to respond, "Don't even ask, because the answer is already no."

And honestly, the answer should be no because she's only twelve. But remember: *connection before correction.* So hear her out. Step into her shoes. Empathize. If you take time to hear her point of view, she might share how all her friends have TikTok, and they make fun of her for not having it.

Resist responding with "Well, if they all walked off a cliff, would you do it?"

Instead, maybe say, "It sounds like you're really frustrated because a lot of your friends have this app and you don't."

"Yeah, I am," she might reply.

"And to make matters worse," you continue, "they tease you for it."

"Yeah."

Then you keep showing empathy by saying, "I'm so sorry they're treating you that way. That's unfair."

But here's where it becomes difficult for many parents. Because the natural place to go from this point is to either give in and let your kid have something that might not be good for her or drop a bomb and tell her no.

### 4. Ask, "What Do You Think Is Best?"

Instead, ask, "What do you think is best?" When you aren't sure how to respond in a situation, ask your kids what they'd do. This is a great way to buy yourself some time.

Perhaps your fourteen-year-old son is asking if he can buy a video game that seems violent to you, and yet most of his church friends play it. You're not sure what to do.

After listening to him and empathizing with his point of view, ask him this question: "So if your fourteen-year-old son asked if he could play this game, how do you think you'd respond?"

I've used this strategy with my own kids more times than I can count. It's nice because life is full of messy moments where the answer isn't clear to our kids. By asking them what's right, we're challenging them to reflect on their personal values and make a wise decision. After all, aren't they going to have to do this on their own someday in a college dorm or an army barracks fifteen hundred miles from home? Wouldn't it be nice to let your kids start practicing now while they're still under your guidance?

### 5. Delay Correction and Decisions

When your kids share what they would do in the situation, resist the urge to set boundaries or impose a decision right away. Instead, take time to consider your kids' perspectives and feelings.

Be honest with your kids and tell them, "This is a lot to think about. And I really want to consider what you've told me. So give me a few days to research this, think it over, and pray."

Then do just that. Research the topic or issue, think it over, and pray specifically, *God, please help me do the right thing. Help me consider the views and feelings of my child. Give me wisdom. Help my child be receptive to my decision. And help me respond well in the moment.*

## A Balancing Act

These five steps have helped me prioritize connection *before* correction. Connection and correction almost seem at odds with each other. We love our kids so much that we want to give them everything they desire, but we don't want to give them something that hurts them. The problem is, kids don't like rules, even loving limits. So parents constantly struggle to balance bonding and boundaries.

No one explains this tension better than Dr. Dan Allender in his book *How Children Raise Parents*. Dan focuses on two key questions our kids ask:

1. Do you love me?
2. Can I do whatever I want?

A loving parent answers those questions this way:

1. Unequivocally yes.
2. Unequivocally no.

And therein lies the tension. Love and limits. Bonding and boundaries. Connection and correction.

Which side of the scale do you gravitate toward? Do you tend to focus on love, bonding, and connection or limits, boundaries, and correction?

If you find yourself leaning toward the correction side of the scale, I'd encourage you to discover ways you can make connection with your children a priority this week. Here are just a few ideas:

- Take each of your kids out for a treat, just the two of you. Use this as a time to ask questions about the things your son or daughter enjoys, and then listen to the thoughts and feelings your child shares.

- Walk into your kid's room, lie down on the floor next to your child, and ask, "So what was the best part of your day today?" Or, "What's one thing you wish I understood about you?" And then just listen.

- If your kid is playing video games or watching YouTube videos, join in. Resist the urge to ask how many minutes of screen time your daughter or son has racked up. Instead ask, "Can I join you?"

Be proactive about connection this week.

## Time for Correction

So when do we correct our children? When do we actually sit down with them and tell them the bad news: "Sorry, no phone in the bedroom"?

Some of you might be great about connecting, but you aren't very good about correcting. As you're reading this book, you might be thinking, *Uh-oh, I've already let my kids have waaaaay too much freedom.*

How can we introduce some loving limits?

What limits do our kids actually need?

This is what we'll discuss in the rest of this book. When you read a chapter that piques your interest, practice what you've learned. Create a climate of comfortable conversation in your home. Bring up the issue at a family gathering. Break the ice with a fun question, then read a noteworthy study or paragraph to your kids and ask your kids' opinions. Listen; don't lecture. Just ask questions. Step into your kids' shoes and try to understand their viewpoints and feelings. Resist criticizing your kids' responses. Instead, ask what they think is best. How would they solve the problem at hand? Delay correction and decisions. Actually walk away. Don't rush to set boundaries or impose a decision right away. Tell your kids you need some time to think and pray about the situation.

Then, eventually, when you finish this book, set a time to talk about what you've read and make some decisions about screens. Give your kids advance notice. You might say, "This Thursday we're going to our favorite pizza place. While we're enjoying our pizza, we'll talk about our screens and make some decisions about how our family can become screenwise." (And yes, at the end of the book, I'll talk a little about what that pizza "meeting" might look like.)

Don't be surprised if your kids aren't thrilled about a family gathering where they know you'll establish screen limits.

One of the best ways to prepare for that family pizza gathering is to begin connecting with your kids one-on-one each week and talking about different issues. That's why I wrote *The Teen's Guide to Face-to-Face Connections in a Screen-to-Screen World*, with discussion questions at the end of each chapter. You can read through the book with your kids and discuss issues together.

Don't expect your kids to understand why they shouldn't have their phones in their bedrooms if they've never peeked at the research on the connection between screens in the bedroom and loss of sleep and depression. But if you connect with your kids weekly and spend time reading about and discussing these issues, you can invite them to share their informed opinions.

*Connection before correction.*

*Love before limits.*

*Bonding before boundaries.*

So what are some of the helpful boundaries our kids might need?

In the next chapter, I'll answer the most common question I'm asked at my parenting workshops.

## Discussion Questions

1. Which do you do more as a parent: correct or connect? Which would your kids say you do more?

2. Jonathan said, "Correction is ineffective without connection." Explain.

3. Jonathan shared important advice from Deuteronomy 6:6-7 that included specific examples of how we can engage our kids in meaningful conversations each day. What similar advice does Psalm 78:1-7 provide?

4. What would happen in your home if you resisted lecturing and instead asked your kids their opinions about screens, social media, and entertainment?

5. What is the benefit of delaying correction and decisions and giving yourself time to research an issue and pray?

6. In what settings can you practice the five steps to placing connection before correction, starting with a family gathering this week?

## CHAPTER 3

# What Age?

*The perfect time to give your kids a screen*

*(and what to do if you already did)*

I HEAR IT EVERYWHERE I SPEAK.

"At what age should I get my kid a phone?"

"At what age should I let my kids be on social media?"

"What if I wanted to wait to give my kids a screen, but their school already issued them one?"

*Sigh.*

Screens sure haven't made parenting any easier.

So what is the perfect age to give your kids a screen?

## Parental Peer Pressure

If you haven't given your kids a screen yet, the pressure is on. Even if they don't have a phone or tablet, chances are their friends already have screens. As I write this, 89 percent of teenagers (ages thirteen to seventeen) have smartphones.[1] This is weird, because if your teenagers don't have phones yet, I'm pretty sure they tell you, "Aaaaall of my friends have smartphones." (You probably should resist the temptation to respond, "Actually, only 89 percent of your friends have smartphones.")

The large number of kids getting phones before they're even teen-agers is becoming less and less surprising. Recently I was hanging out with sixth, seventh, and eighth graders on a middle school campus near my house, and it sure seemed like "aaaaall" of them had smartphones. (I know, I sound exactly like your kid.)

In fact, I was talking with thirteen of these students in a class-room at an after-school program. These were eleven-, twelve-, and thirteen-year-olds.

I wrote my phone number on the whiteboard and said, "Everyone whip out your phones."

And count 'em . . . *all thirteen* pulled out a smartphone.

Every single one of them!

This seems bizarre when you consider what I shared in the first chapter about the number of kids who have smartphones:

- 53 percent of eleven-year-olds
- 69 percent of twelve-year-olds
- 72 percent of thirteen-year-olds

Nope. Not in this group.

One hundred percent of them had smartphones.

So think how your own twelve-year-old is feeling at school every day. Your son or daughter probably feels as if "aaaaall" the other kids have smartphones.

I decided to play a game with these middle schoolers and see what I could learn.

"We're gonna play speed text," I told them. "The first one to text me what I ask for wins a point. The first one to ten points gets a gift card to Starbucks."

(Yes, I bribe middle school kids with caffeine. Parents love me.)

Kids were already entering my number in their phones and sitting there poised, waiting for my first question.

"Send me your first and last name and a selfie," I said.

They all held up their phones, tapped off a quick selfie, and began typing furiously.

My phone blew up. *Ding. Ding. Ding . . .*

Within two seconds, I had thirteen texts with hilarious pics of each of their faces.

I kept going. "Send me a picture of your shoes."

*Ding. Ding. Ding. Ding. Ding. Ding . . .*

Nikes. Checkered Vans. More checkered Vans.

"Send me a screenshot of the app you spend the most time on."

*Ding. Ding. Ding. Ding. Ding. Ding . . .*

Again, my phone blew up with pictures of Snapchat, Instagram, TikTok, and some of their favorite mobile games . . .

"Send me a screenshot of the most recent song you were listening to."

*Ding. Ding. Ding. Ding. Ding. Ding . . .*

That question was pretty revealing. Kids don't really stop and think when they're playing this kind of game. So I was receiving raw screenshots of the songs they had just been playing through their earbuds moments before. Mostly songs Mom or Dad didn't know about. (You can learn a lot about kids from their phones.)

A kid named Jordan was the first to ten. I gave him a fist bump and the Starbucks card and then began asking the class questions.

"So when did you get your phones?"

Kids didn't hesitate to answer.

"Last year."

"I've had mine for a couple years now."

"My older brother got a new one, so I got his old one."

"I noticed many of you have Snapchat and Instagram. So when did you first get social media?"

Kids shouted answers, almost bragging.

"It's the first thing I downloaded."

"Since fifth grade."

Then I asked a question that surprised them a little bit. "How many of you knew you were going to have to lie about your age to get on social media?" (Most of these kids had just admitted they downloaded social media apps before age thirteen. You have to be thirteen to sign up for any of these apps.)

They all smiled and looked at each other for a moment, as if they were wondering, *Should I tell him?* But they did.

"My sister told me I'd have to."

"I didn't know until I tried. But it was simple. You just type in a different year."

"I used my same birthday but a different year. That way people still know my birthday."

Then I asked one final question.

"How many of your parents know you lied about your age?"

After just fifteen minutes interacting with this particular group of young people, it immediately became apparent: These kids all had smartphones, they spent countless hours soaking in mobile entertainment, and they were all on social media. Their parents also knew very little about what they were doing on their phones every day.

Maybe that's why parents are so quick to hand their kids a screen. They have no idea what they're actually giving their kids. That's why I typically spend the first half of a parenting workshop giving parents a very realistic glimpse of what's on their kids' screens. I show them a few snippets from the top songs, games, and videos. Then I'll show them real comments that have been posted and predatory behaviors that happen on social media when kids leave their privacy settings on public. As I mentioned earlier, an overwhelming majority of young people use the public setting because they want more followers.

After showing parents all of this, I ask, "Do your kids have their privacy settings so *anyone* can see their profile?"

I can see the looks on their faces. Moms and dads have no idea, and now they're thinking, *Why did I give my fifth grader a phone?*

But some parents didn't even make that decision themselves. I talk with divorced parents frequently, and some of them tell me that the other spouse gave their kids a phone without discussing it with them first. No divorced parent wants to be the bad guy and say, "Not in this house!" They know that their kids will simply say, "Well, then I want to go live with Dad!"

Sometimes schools issue screens, and not just during global pandemics. Some schools issue fourth and fifth graders iPads or other tablets.

Parents always ask me, "Can my kid get into any trouble on these screens?"

It depends. I've spoken with several people who work in technology for school districts all over the country. Most of them are pretty confident that kids *can't* wander into too much trouble while they're connected on the school networks. But when kids bring the devices home—and most do—they're often free to browse wherever they want, depending on the home connection. (More on this in our chapter about parental controls.)

So here are the key questions we'll talk about in this chapter:

- What is the right age to give kids their own phones?
- What about other screens?
- What if your kids already have screens, and you're having second thoughts?

Let's see if we can answer them.

## What Is the Right Age to Give Kids Their Own Phones?

I think it's always helpful to look at what the experts are saying about this issue. These are the people who really know the ins and outs of technology.

In a recent interview with *The Mirror*, Microsoft founder Bill Gates revealed that he didn't let any of his three children get a smartphone until they were fourteen and in high school.[2] He also doesn't allow screens at the dinner table, and he limits screen time for his youngest child before bedtime.

Like Gates, CEO Jim Steyer of Common Sense Media didn't give his kids smartphones until high school, "after they [had] learned restraint and the value of face-to-face communication."[3]

I know what you're thinking. *Is waiting until high school realistic when all my kids' friends are getting devices younger?* I hear you, and I agree it's frustrating. But if you research this topic, you'll encounter the words *high school* again and again. The age level is about the same as learning to drive.

Greg Lukianoff, coauthor of *The Coddling of the American Mind: How Good Intentions and Bad Ideas Are Setting Up a Generation for Failure*, speaks about this topic not only in his book but in countless follow-up articles. In one of those articles, he was very specific about age, especially after examining extensive research on the effects social media has had on kids, particularly on young girls:

> The case is now much stronger that girls who become heavy users of social media have worse mental health. . . . Parents should try to delay the day when their kids (especially daughters) get accounts on Instagram and other platforms where people rate them and comment on their looks and their posts. They should talk with their children about the dangers

of these platforms, and they should consider tight time limits on their use (such as one or at most two hours a day). School districts should help parents by strongly suggesting the norm that *no kids get social media accounts* until high school, to avoid the fear of exclusion that leads many parents to allow their kids to lie about their age and open an Instagram account in sixth grade, or even fifth grade. Middle school is already so hard on kids, and social media makes the worst parts even worse.[4] (Emphasis added)

There are those words again: *high school*. I hope school districts take Lukianoff's advice and recommend that parents create a norm of delaying when kids get devices. Because right now, kids who don't have phones feel excluded. Middle school kids without phones feel pressure from their friends to have them so they can get on social media with everyone else.

But peer pressure doesn't change the opinions of mental-health experts. A few years ago, the *New York Times* ran an article asking, "What's the right age for a child to get a smartphone?"

"The takeaway will not please smartphone makers," the author concluded. "The longer you wait to give your children a smartphone, the better."[5]

Jesse Weinberger, author and internet safety speaker, says, "The longer you keep Pandora's box shut, the better off you are."[6]

Simon Sinek, author and professor at Columbia University, speaks to this in his YouTube talk about smartphone addiction and the dopamine hits social media provides:

Parents have to intervene. We have to stop giving our kids free access to social media and phones at young ages. They are not ready for it. Their minds cannot cope with the dopamine.[7]

Dopamine is a chemical released in the reward centers of the brain that helps you remember what feels good when you do certain activities, like taking drugs or playing the slots in Vegas. The next time that particular activity is dangled before your senses, dopamine gives you a rush, triggering the anticipation of good feelings and fueling a desire to engage in the activity even more. For that reason, dopamine-triggering behaviors easily become a habit, which is why most studies show that social media leads to more social media. (And since I'm not a neuroscientist, I'm going to leave it at that.)

Tristan Harris, a former design ethicist at Google, says that phones are designed to be addictive.[8] Citing Harris, Humanity Forward founder Andrew Yang says, "We're all walking around with slot machines in our pockets. We don't let our children into casinos; we should be just as wary of letting these casinos into our children's hands."[9]

Young people don't recognize these dangers. That's why the advice I give is similar to the advice of these tech experts: Don't be in a hurry to give your kids a phone. Only give them a device this powerful when you can invest the time in teaching them how to use it responsibly. Don't just toss them a device with the excuse that they probably understand how to use it better than you do. Sure, they might know how to operate it, but most young people haven't thought through the ramifications of *whom they friend, what they post,* and *where they navigate.* These are very difficult decisions for a child.

> *Only give them a device this powerful when you can invest the time in teaching them how to use it responsibly.*

Some parents will press me for a number.

"What age?" they ask.

"It depends on the kid," I always respond. "It's about maturity more than age."

But for some reason, people always insist I give them some sort of broad-stroke average age.

"When are they typically mature enough?" they ask.

So I'll tell them, "Bare minimum, thirteen years old."

Why? Because one of the first things kids download on their phones is social media, and you can't be on social media until you're thirteen without lying about your age.

This makes the social media debate pretty clear cut.

If they want to know why, tell them it's the law. It's called COPPA, or the Federal Trade Commission's Children's Online Privacy Protection Act. And even if your kids have never heard of the law, they know about it. Because when anyone tries to sign up for Snapchat, Instagram, TikTok, Twitter, or any other social media app they desire, they first have to enter their birth date. If a kid is under thirteen, the app will reply, "Sorry, you are not old enough to use this app."

That's because COPPA doesn't allow websites or social media apps to collect personal information from anyone under thirteen without parental consent.[10]

Does it work? Does it prohibit kids under thirteen from getting on social media?

Not in the slightest.

That's because no one's policing it. Especially parents. Every time I'm on a middle school campus, I see countless eleven- and twelve-year-olds on Snapchat and Instagram, because they simply lied about their age to sign up.

So the pressure is on. When you tell your kid, "Sorry, you can't download Snapchat because you're not thirteen yet. It's the law," your kid is going to argue, "But Chris has Snapchat, and he's eleven!"

Your kid isn't lying.

That's one of the reasons why it's better not to give your kids a phone until thirteen years of age or later. The temptation to lie about

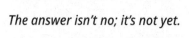

*The answer isn't no; it's not yet.*

their age to get on social media is just too great.

Every weekend at my workshops, I talk with parents who gave their kids a phone at age eleven or twelve. And they all quickly discovered that their kids immediately wanted Snapchat or Instagram so they could communicate with their friends.

"Why have a phone if you can't have Instagram?" kids say.

Even if Mom or Dad says no, many kids will disobey and download social media without their parents' knowledge. So delay device ownership.

The answer isn't no; it's not yet.

## What about Other Screens?

"Oh, I would never give my kids a phone," one mom told me.

Wait for it.

I knew it was coming.

"I got them an iPad."

Whenever a parent tells me this, I try to be understanding, so I just walk them through the logic.

Think about this for a second. What's the difference between a phone and a tablet?

Besides portability and size, there's basically one difference: *cellular connection.*

In other words, smartphones automatically have a cellular connection, but most tablets have only Wi-Fi connectability. However, with a tablet, your kids can still download all the same social media, play the same mobile games, watch the same YouTube videos (but on a bigger screen), stream the same movies (in greater detail), and listen to the same music.

If your kids have a tablet without a cellular connection, the only thing they *can't* do is put their tablet in a pocket, go out in the middle of a field, and connect.

- They can still connect to everything at home through Wi-Fi.
- They can still connect at school and almost any public place.
- They can even still connect in the middle of nowhere by using their friends' hot spots.

Bottom line: if your kids want an iPad or tablet of any kind, use the same discretion you'd use if they wanted a phone. Consider these questions:

- Are my kids mature enough to begin making these decisions about content?

- Do I want my kids to start feeling the pressure to be on social media?

- Am I ready for the battles they will fight over screen time and bringing their tablets into the bedroom at night?

- Do I want to monitor the apps my kids are downloading, the connections they're making, and the content they're streaming?

- Am I ready to begin teaching my kids the responsibility that comes with tablet ownership . . . or do I just "throw them the keys"?

It's not that screens are bad or evil. Owning a screen is just like owning a car. It requires taking on a lot of responsibility.

But screens will also change the interaction in your home.

Last spring I taught a parenting workshop in the South. Loretta Lynn territory. (I had some amazing barbecue on the way there.) A mom approached me after the workshop and told me a story about her son.

"I caved and bought him an iPad," she began.

"When?" I asked.

"Last year when he turned eight. And slowly he began to change."

"How so?"

"It just started to absorb him," she explained. "Every time we'd try to talk with him or call him down to dinner, he gave us attitude. It was a fight to get him to put down the screen."

"So what did you do?"

"One day he was being so disrespectful, I just took it away."

"How'd that work out?"

"He threw a fit. Day one, he screamed and yelled. Day two, he argued and fought. Day three, he just moped around like he was on death row."

I laughed.

"But then something interesting happened," she said. "He slowly emerged from his bedroom like he used to and started hanging around with us again."

"That's cool," I said.

"About three weeks passed," she continued. "And I had told him I was taking his iPad away for a month. But we were supposed to go on a trip, just him, me, and my mom—his grandma. We do this trip every year."

"That sounds nice."

"So I told my mom that I took away his iPad, and she said, 'For the trip? Aren't you going to give it back to him? All that time in the car. What is he gonna do?'"

"So what did you do?" I asked.

"I *didn't* give it back. He had to ride with us without it, and"—here she paused, and her eyes teared up. I gave her a moment.

"Sorry," she said. "But as we hit the open road, he said, 'Mom, look at that old barn. Look at those baby cows. Look at those trees.' It was like he had never seen a stupid tree before!"

She wiped her tears with her sleeve. "I'm never giving that thing back to him."

Some kids just aren't ready for the responsibility that comes with having a screen.

## What If Your Kids Already Have Screens, and You're Having Second Thoughts?

Parents always ask me, "What if I already gave my kid a phone, and now I'm having second thoughts? What now? Should I take it away?"

Here's one of those instances where you want to be very careful not to overreact and just yank your kid's device away. That's like telling your kid, "We're going to Disneyland!" but then after buying the tickets and walking one hundred feet into the park, you look around skeptically at the crowd and announce, "Sorry, we're going home!"

This decision will have a psychological impact!

"Remember when Dad took us to Disneyland for two minutes?" they'll say.

Kids love their screens. Big-time. According to a number of surveys, it's their most prized possession. So think through this decision shrewdly. And make sure you and your spouse are in agreement (even Stepmom, Stepdad, the ex—everyone), or your kids will start playing the adults against each other.

Before you take screens away from your kids, consider a few options (and age is a huge factor). If you already handed your eight- or ten-year-old a screen, then, sure, you could explain some of the dangers and take it away. But if you do, prepare for battle. This is something you gave your child and then revoked. That's tough on a kid.

A shrewder approach might be to sit down and talk with your kids about the dangers and then just set some very strict boundaries with the screens, letting your kids know, "If you violate any of these rules even once, say good-bye to your screen until age thirteen." Then if your kids violate the screen rules, it's much easier to take their devices away (not without whining and complaining), because at least they understand that it's the punishment for violating the rules.

While you're at it, access the parental controls on your kids' devices and block out many, if not most, of the dangers. No, I'm not talking about filtering software. I'm talking about fully lobotomizing their phones, setting secure passwords, blocking the ability to download apps or social media without a password, and thinking of ways to limit screen time to a minimum. (We'll talk more about screen-time limits in an upcoming chapter.) Minimizing screen time is better than taking your kid's phone away and announcing, "Sorry. My bad. I should never have given you this phone in the first place."

For example, if you gave your fourteen-year-old a phone, and you're just scared because of all the dangers, in 95 percent of cases, I wouldn't take it away. In fact, I would consider giving my fourteen-year-old a phone if he or she asked for one (but I wouldn't bring it up). That way, teens can start learning to be responsible before they leave the home.

If your teens break a rule with their devices or prove to be irresponsible, sure, you might ground them without their phones for a period of time or until they prove they're responsible. But taking away a phone just because you're worried could have very negative consequences. I've witnessed hundreds of parents overreact and become too restrictive with their teens. Typically, I've seen several negative results:

- Teens distance themselves from their parents—"Dad just doesn't understand." So they look to other role models from whom to glean values and learn how to make decisions. The parents' impact is severely impaired.

- Teens cheat and find a way to access screens when Mom and Dad aren't around. Rule of thumb: the tighter parents squeeze, the more the kids slip out of their hands.

- Parents panic and tip the scales toward boundaries, and then bonding suffers. Sadly, boundaries don't teach our kids discernment.

You'll hear me say this over and over: Remember to keep your eye on the calendar. Someday your kids will be eighteen and will leave the house, free to download whatever they want. Are you preparing them for that day? Or are you just making every decision for them?

So how can you navigate these conversations?

If you've already given your kids screens, think hard before revoking screen privileges. There are much better ways to protect them. If your kids are ten years old or younger, and you've already given them screens, maybe just use parental controls, screen limits, and guidelines to severely restrict access. (This book will lay out what those guidelines can actually look like.) If your kids are eleven to thirteen, and you've already given them screens, be proactive about connection before correction. They'll appreciate your talking with them rather than just laying down the law.

How do you talk with kids about screen privileges?

Practice the five steps you read about in chapter 2, when you learned how to create a climate of comfortable conversation about these issues:

1. When you read something in this book that piques your interest, bring it up at a family gathering. Break the ice with a fun question. For example, "If there was a power outage and all your screens and devices ran out of battery life, what would be the first thing you'd do for fun?"

PARENTING GENERATION SCREEN

2. Bring up the issue you'd like to talk about by reading a note-worthy paragraph or study. Then ask your kids' opinions. Listen; don't lecture. Just ask questions, such as . . .

   • When did most of your friends get their phones?

   • Why do you think so many tech experts tell parents to wait until their kids get into high school to give them phones?

   • What are some of the things middle school kids would miss if nobody got phones or social media until high school?

   • What problems might actually be avoided if middle school kids didn't get phones or social media until high school?

3. Practice empathy by stepping into your kids' shoes and trying to understand their viewpoints and feelings. Don't criticize their responses; just listen.

4. Ask your kids, "What do you think is best? How would you solve the problem at hand?" Or, in this case, ask, "When do you think parents should allow their kids to get their own phones?"

5. Delay correction or decisions. Actually walk away. Don't rush to set boundaries or impose a decision right away. Tell your kids you need some time to think and pray about the situation.

You might practice these steps over and over as you're reading this book. Then, eventually, when you finish the book, you'll add one final step:

6. Set a time to talk about what you've read and make some decisions about screens. Give your kids advance notice. You might say, "This Thursday we're going out for pizza to talk about how we can become screenwise in this house."

Some of you might still be thinking, *Jonathan, even if I walk through all of these steps, when I finally get to step six, should I take away the screens?*

What if you give your kids a choice?

## The Choice

Don't just lay down the law. Make it a choice. Not any old choice, but a choice with a healthy outcome either way.

I remember talking with a therapist about one of my own kids who was very stubborn and resistant to any kind of rule. If my wife and I set a rule, it seemed as if we were dangling a carrot in front of him and shouting, "Break this rule!"

I'll never forget my counselor's advice. (And yes, I just admitted that my wife, Lori, and I saw a counselor. It was one of the best decisions we ever made for our marriage and our parenting. I wish I had done it sooner.)

She said, "If you have a kid who is pushing against authority, make everything a choice."

"How?" I called her bluff. "What if my kid was spending too much time playing video games?"

"Say to him, 'You've got a choice between two options: you can either keep playing that game system we bought you and abide by our time limits and grade requirements, or you can go get a job and buy your own game system, and then you'll only be limited by the grade requirements we all agreed on.'"

*Pure genius. Give kids a choice.*

This would have been a win-win for our family. Even if my son did choose to get a job and buy his own game system (which would actually demonstrate a lot of drive and follow-through), he'd still have to keep up his grades to keep the privilege. This is Adulting 101. Good stuff.

No matter what situation I shared with my counselor, she was able to come up with a set of choices we could propose to our child.

You can do the same with your kids if you've already given them a phone. You could start off saying, "I've gotta be honest, the more I research some of the distractions screens cause and the dangers on social media . . ."

At this point, your kids' eyes will probably get really big. They might even scream, "Noooooooooo! Don't take away my phone!" They see it coming.

So don't do it. Don't take away their screens. Empower your kids by giving them a choice. Tell them, "So here's what I've decided. You have a choice. I can either take away your phone, and you'll get one when you start high school. It's like driving—and you can't do that until you're sixteen. Or . . . "

They'll be waiting for this "or" because they'd rather do anything but what you just suggested.

So you say, "Or . . . we'll go to breakfast once a week and talk about how to be responsible with your phone. If you meet weekly with me and read a book about becoming screenwise, you can keep your phone."

You're giving your kids the choice between correction or connection. *Ninety-nine* out of one hundred kids will choose connection. (But if your kids choose correction, it's time to reread chapter 2 and begin working on how you connect.)

Sometimes kids won't understand.

Your son may ask, "Why can't I just have the phone? My friend Taylor has a phone, and his parents don't make him do nothing." (Don't hold your kid's grammar against him.)

If he wants to know why, elaborate with this analogy:

Your phone is like a car. Some people learn how to drive a car, obey speed limits, change lanes safely, avoid distractions, and drive to school, church, and Grandma's house. Others drive dangerously, speed, take their eyes off the road, and injure themselves or others. They will eventually lose the privilege of driving. So if you want to drive, you need to wait until you're the right age. You'll have to take a driver's education course, study the driving manual, pass a written test, and even take a behind-the-wheel test. If and only if you prove that you're responsible will you be allowed to drive. But even then, it will be limited at first. You won't drive at night, or blast the radio, or have friends in the car. As you grow more mature and become more experienced, you'll slowly be able to drive later at night and have friends in the car with you. The same will be true of your phone.

Help your kids understand that the greater the privilege, the greater the responsibility. And once they turn fourteen, continue connecting with them and talking about stuff that matters. (I've written quite a few books about this that are just for young people—with discussion questions near the end of each chapter so you can read the book along with them and engage them in meaningful discussions.) Teach your kids discernment in all areas of life.

Isn't that the goal?

## Not Yet

It's intriguing to learn what people in the tech industry do with their own kids. They know the effects technology has on young people, especially social media.

A couple years ago, the *New York Times* released an exposé featuring a bunch of tech-industry executives who live in Silicon Valley.[11] It's ironic, but when these executives (and former executives) of companies such as Facebook, Apple, and Mozilla were interviewed, they said that when they left their homes in the morning, they gave one simple set of instructions to the nannies: "No screens."

And these parents are screen experts!

Chris Anderson of *Wired* magazine said this about screen time:

> On the scale between candy and crack cocaine, it's closer to crack cocaine. . . . We thought we could control it, and this is beyond our power to control. This is going straight to the pleasure centers of the developing brain. This is beyond our capacity as regular parents to understand.[12]

Anderson didn't give his kids phones until the summer before they started high school. He didn't let them on social media until they were thirteen, and he didn't allow phones in their bedrooms.

These are extremely helpful guidelines from a guy who really understands technology.

In the next chapter, we'll look a little closer at why that last rule he mentioned—no phones in the bedroom—is so important.

## Discussion Questions

1. Why do you think so many tech experts, including Jonathan, wait until their kids are thirteen or fourteen before giving them phones, when most parents give their kids phones at the average age of ten?

2. What are parents communicating to their kids who are younger than thirteen when they let them lie about their age to get on social media?

3. What would happen if every parent in your community listened to Jonathan's advice: "Only give your kids a device this powerful when you can invest the time in teaching them how to use it responsibly"?

4. If you gave screens to your kids when they were younger (before high school), were you surprised at Jonathan's advice to "think through the decision shrewdly" before you take away their phones? Did you like any of the alternatives he suggested? Which one did you like most?

5. What's the benefit of empowering your kids by giving them a choice, such as the choice to have their phones taken away or to meet together weekly to read through a book and discuss being wise with screens?

6. How do you think your kids would respond if you compared using a phone to driving a car?

7. How can you begin engaging your kids in these types of conversations this week?

## CHAPTER 4

# "Mom, Can I Have My Phone in My Bedroom?"

*The link between screens, sleep loss, and depression . . .*
*and what you can do about it*

"TIME FOR BED."

"Okay." Sarah complied without any argument.

Sarah's mom thought, *That was easy.* She didn't question her daughter's unusual behavior until a week later when Sarah slept through her alarm again.

Sarah McKinsey had just turned twelve, and her parents had finally caved and bought her the smartphone she'd been begging for.

Sarah plugged it in and set it on her nightstand every night right before bed.

"I use it as my alarm clock," she reasoned. But waking up was proving quite difficult.

"Come on, Sarah. Wakey, wakey!" Mrs. McKinsey said, opening the blinds and letting the sunlight pour in.

"Mom," Sarah whined. "Just ten more minutes."

"You said that ten minutes ago. You can't keep hitting your snooze button."

The battles became more frequent, and Sarah became volatile. After school just two days later, Sarah's mom reminded her that they'd all be going to her aunt's house for dinner that night. Sarah blew a gasket.

"What?" she screamed, throwing her backpack across the room. "I hate going to Aunt Lisa's. Why do I have to go?"

"What's wrong with you lately, Sarah?" her mom asked.

The battles continued.

Three nights later after Sarah's dad finished some late-night work in the den, he shut off the lights to hit the hay. Walking down the hallway, he saw a slight glow coming from under Sarah's door.

He glanced at his watch: 12:42 a.m.

He quietly walked toward his daughter's door. The floor creaked in its usual spot. He opened her door gently and peeked in.

Nothing.

Her room was completely dark, and Sarah was lying still in her bed. He walked over to her and kissed her softly on the cheek.

*Bzzzzzzzzzzzzz.*

Mr. McKinsey froze. He couldn't tell where the sound was coming from.

*Bzzzzzzzzzzzzz.*

Then he spotted the phone on Sarah's nightstand. He picked it up and saw two messages on the screen. Both of them were from a guy named Dillon on Sarah's favorite social media app.

**Dillon:** IDK. Did u talk with her?

**Dillon:** U there?

Her dad scrolled up to keep reading when Sarah opened her eyes, alert as ever.

"Dad, don't read that."

"Ah. So were you just playing possum?"

"Give me that," she demanded, completely ignoring his question.

"No," Mr. McKinsey said. "I can't believe you're up messaging your friends at this time of night!"

Sarah scoffed. "Dad, it's no big deal."

That was the night World War III began. Ask anyone in the McKinsey house, and they'll tell you.

This battle isn't uncommon. Young people want their phones in their bedrooms, and they don't care what anyone else has to say about it.

The McKinseys never saw it coming. They never fathomed that Sarah would stay up all hours of the night, messaging her friends on social media.

And being completely fair, no one had ever warned them that phones are by far the biggest cause of kids losing out on needed sleep each night. (And they are.) So by the time it came to their attention, Sarah's heels were dug in deep.

Most parents don't realize how much a phone distracts their kids from sleep. Maybe because we didn't experience that same temptation when we were kids. Maybe we tried to stay up late reading or listening to music with our headphones on. But we sure didn't have social media, YouTube, Google, Netflix, gaming, or Pornhub—all just a tap away on one simple device.

But let's not be quick to villainize the smartphone. It isn't the only screen keeping kids up at night.

My friend's son Bodie was only thirteen when he got his first laptop, a great tool for school—that's what his parents said anyway. Maybe that's why they didn't think it was a big deal to let Bodie keep the laptop in his room at night.

Bodie's dad didn't find anything amiss for months, until he happened to look at his wireless streaming activity, which detailed the times of day when the most streaming took place. The first thing he noticed was that Bodie had maxed out his high-speed streaming two weeks into the month. The family's wireless service provided tiered service, which slowed down after a certain tier limit was reached. Bodie hit that limit before anyone else. Not only that, but he primarily streamed from 10:00 p.m. to about 2:00 a.m. most of the time.

My friend had actually set controls on his home router to turn off the kids' access after 9:00 p.m. But what he hadn't foreseen was that Bodie could use his phone's hot spot to connect to the internet. If Bodie's dad had ever walked into his son's room late at night, which he didn't, he would have found Bodie wearing a headset and gaming with a bunch of friends.

When my friend asked his son why he did it, Bodie answered, "Because I always have trouble going to sleep."

And then he declared, "What's the big deal?"

That's what most young people today will say: "It's no big deal."

So is it? And if so, how can we talk with our kids about it?

## The Common Denominator

If I could choose only one rule for kids growing up today, it would be, hands down, *no* screens in the bedroom. That one simple guardrail would solve innumerable problems.

No, this isn't an oversimplification. It's just that after thirty years of working with young people, raising three kids of my own, working in social research, and hearing parents share countless problems and frustrations with their kids, I've learned that screens in the bedroom are a common denominator for trouble.

Whether it's meeting strangers on social media, playing video games well into the night, or watching pornographic videos, whenever kids confess engaging in one of these activities to me, no question, it happened late at night on a screen in their bedrooms.

In fact, whenever I'm taking questions from parents in my workshops or on the radio, I feel like a broken record at times.

They'll tell me about some random struggle with one of their kids. Then they'll say, ". . . and the next thing I knew, I discovered Jordan was doing this regularly."

Without fail, I'll ask, "Does Jordan have his phone in his bedroom at night?"

"Yes," they'll tell me.

Then I'll reply, "Collect it from him at bedtime and charge it in your room at night. Next question."

(Okay, I don't really respond that abruptly. But I'm tempted to.)

In my line of work, I've seen it again and again. While working on a previous book that required hundreds of hours of cyberbullying research, I kept encountering the same phrase: "My kid was being tormented all through the night on social media by cruel messages, posts, and comments."

*All through the night.*

Many times these kids went into a downward spiral of depression not because of the bullying but simply because they were losing sleep.

Lack of sleep is one of the primary factors associated with depression, and vice versa (hence the all-too-common downward spiral). In fact, in a study of nearly twenty-eight thousand high school students, researchers discovered that the odds of teens feeling sad or hopeless increased by 38 percent for each hour of lost sleep, and the risk of attempted suicide increased 58 percent.[1]

*Each hour of lost sleep bumps up the chances of your kid feeling hopeless by almost 40 percent.*

Read that again. Each hour of lost sleep bumps up the chances of your kid feeling hopeless by almost 40 percent.

And what is the number one culprit keeping kids up at night?

Screens.

Two of the few things all experts actually agree on are *avoiding screen time immediately before bed and keeping screens out of the bedroom.*

Unfortunately, most parents aren't listening.

## Phones in the Bedroom

Long before young people had smartphones, the American Academy of Pediatrics was recommending that parents remove TVs and internet from kids' bedrooms.[2] Now, your kids have TV, social media, music, and texting on *just one device*—and your pediatrician's advice hasn't changed.

When the majority of American kids ended up with smartphones in their pockets, pediatricians strongly recommended that "children not sleep with devices in their bedrooms, including TVs, computers, and smartphones. [They should also] avoid exposure to devices or screens for 1 hour before bedtime."[3]

Do you wonder how many moms and dads actually listened to this advice?

Only about 20 percent.

In 2019, an eye-opening study surveyed twelve- to eighteen-year-olds living at home. Researchers specifically asked how many teens brought their phones into the bedroom each night and how often they checked them. The survey revealed that 79 percent of teenagers bring their phones into the bedroom each night, with 68 percent keeping their phones within reach, including 29 percent who actually sleep with their devices in their beds.[4]

So why do so many parents allow their kids to keep their devices in the bedrooms when their family doctors have been saying no screens in the bedroom for literally decades? Perhaps it's because 74 percent of American adults sleep with their own phones or keep them within arm's reach.[5]

Maybe it's because, once again, the pressure is on. When 89 percent of your daughter's friends have smartphones,[6] and 79 percent of them bring their phones into their bedrooms every night, your daughter might seriously wonder why you have such unfair and archaic screen rules.

So let me ask the question teens are wondering about: Is there a chance loony alarmists and doomsayers are just making an issue out of something that is truly "no big deal"?

Sorry, the facts prove it's a very big deal. Pediatricians actually know what they're talking about. There really isn't any debate about it. The more time young people spend on screens, the less they sleep. And when kids bring their screens into their bedrooms, sleep suffers even more, and the consequences of poor sleep are colossal and costly.

These are important issues to talk about with your kids, and as we've already discussed, they don't want to hear a simple "Because I said so" or, in this case, "Because your doctor said so!" This is another opportunity to dialogue with them about the reasons behind the decision so they can be equipped to make the same decision for themselves when they're out on their own.

So let's look at some of these reasons, beginning with exactly how screens affect sleep.

## Do Screens Really Affect My Kids' Sleep?

Everyone agrees that teenagers should sleep about nine hours a night. Younger kids need considerably more sleep. But currently, almost half of American teenagers average fewer than seven hours of sleep per night.

When did this happen?

Let me give you the history of smartphones in four sentences: In the early 2000s, kids had plain old cell phones. If they wanted to be on social media, they did it on a computer. But then the first iPhone was released in January of 2007. America immediately fell in love with smartphones, and by 2012, more than half of teenagers already had them in their pockets.

That's when the shift happened.

Between 2012 and 2015, the number of teens who got fewer than seven hours of sleep per night increased by 22 percent.[7]

I look at these types of statistics a lot. The numbers change 3 percent, 5 percent . . . and at times, maybe even 10 percent. But a 22 percent jump only occurs when a new variable is introduced into the scenario. And 2012 actually introduced several new variables: It was the year when a majority of kids became smartphone owners, Snapchat was released, and Instagram exploded in popularity.

Now that kids carry screens, and social media, around with them 24/7, almost half of them sleep fewer than seven hours per night (which is actually a 58 percent increase in the number of teens who slept fewer than seven hours in 1991).[8]

That's a lot of tired kids!

So how are screens keeping them up at night?

## 1. Screens Delay When Your Kids Go to Sleep

First, let me just quickly address the almost insignificant fact about screens: the blue light they emit is known to hurt our bodies' ability to sleep. Why is this insignificant? Because it's an easy fix. Chances are, your kids already know about this and consider it "no big deal," since all they need to do is switch their phones to "Night Shift" or "Night Light" mode to kill the blue light. Countless online sources explain how to do this.

Your kids are right—the blue-light issue is an easy fix. But the loss of sleep young people are experiencing is from more than just the lights their screens emit. Even without the blue light, screens engage our kids' brains, causing them to be alert and stimulated, which makes sleep more difficult.

The more our kids become engaged with screens, the worse they're sleeping.

That's why your pediatrician is instructed to advise you and your child, "No screens one hour before bedtime." Yet, an overwhelming majority of parents ignore this advice.

Not only do 79 percent of teenagers bring their phones into their bedrooms each night, but, as the same study revealed, 70 percent use their devices within thirty minutes of lights out.[9] And then they lie there in bed with their minds racing.

Social media is probably one of the biggest culprits that keep kids awake at night—by design. No, it's not like evil app developers necessarily wanted to keep our kids awake so they would perform poorly at school the next day, but these developers definitely did create the app to engage kids, stimulate their brains, and reward them periodically to keep them engrossed. Scrolling through social media is known to stimulate dopamine in their brains, telling them, "Hey, man, this is gonna feel good!" And that anticipation typically increases wakefulness.

The same is true of looking at internet pornography. When a kid encounters pornography repeatedly, the mere anticipation of the visuals gives him a dopamine rush before any physical pleasure even takes place. I intentionally say *him* not because girls don't ever look at porn, but compared to young boys, fewer than half the number of young girls engage in frequent porn viewing. The Barna Group conducted a survey to find out how many "practicing" and "not practicing" Christians from thirteen to twenty-four years of age seek out porn "at least once a month." Here are the results:[10]

- 72 percent of "not practicing" Christian males
- 41 percent of "practicing" Christian males
- 36 percent of "not practicing" Christian females
- 13 percent of "practicing" Christian females

Let those numbers sink in for a moment. Even if your son goes to church and loves Jesus, *41 percent of "practicing" Christian males from 13 to 24 years of age frequently seek out porn.*

The lure of porn is commonplace today, with countless gateways. Consider YouTube, a favorite online destination for young people. Even if your kids are watching an innocent video, when that video ends, YouTube "kindly" suggests more videos your kids might like, and every once in a while, one of those "suggestions" features a slightly alluring image. And as many of you know, tapping on that video link can lead viewers down a rabbit trail to porn.

In short, porn is a huge temptation for young people today, especially males. Having a phone in their bedrooms increases accessibility, with less accountability. And the more kids view porn, the more they desire it. Internet porn has a way of leading to even more internet porn.

It's the same with video games. Unlike movies or TV programs, video games are interactive. Most studies show that playing video games before bed not only increases "sleep-onset latency" (the time it takes kids to fall asleep), but it also amps kids up so much, it hurts their ability to transition into a deep sleep.[11]

*One in three teenagers wake up in the middle of the night to check their phone.*

What does all this mean?

Our doctors are right when they advise us, "Stop using screens before bedtime. It will hurt your sleep."

## 2. Screens Interrupt Your Kids' Sleep.

Screens not only delay *when* our kids go to sleep; they also interrupt sleep throughout the night. One in three teenagers wake up in the middle of the night to check their phone.[12]

Think about that for a second. If you have three kids with phones in their bedrooms, then statistically, one of them is getting up to check a notification or jump on social media real quick in the middle of the night.

Ask yourself, *Would this affect my sleep?*

You have to step into their world for a moment to try to understand. For most kids today, "likes" and followers are everything. In a world where almost nine out of ten young people (86 percent) want to become social media influencers,[13] social status is everything. (We'll spend plenty of time diving into the influencer phenomenon in upcoming chapters.) So if your kids post a new video right before bed, chances are they'll wake up during the night to check likes and comments.

And how do you think it's going to affect their sleep when they don't get as many likes as they wanted?

Will their minds become engaged when they read a negative comment trashing their video? (Sadly, internet "trolls" are everywhere. These people love to provoke a response with their critical or cruel comments, like a fisherman trolling for a catch.)

Far too many kids tend to wake up and peek at their phones when they have them in their bedrooms. As I've already mentioned, one in three teenagers (statistically 36 percent) wake up at least once during the night to check their mobile devices.[14] But honestly, I think that number has grown since 2019. Social media has become even more engrossing. I've met numerous kids who claim they're up "all through the night" checking notifications. Some almost seem to brag about insomnia.

Like Adam.

Adam's grades were dropping, he was having outbursts at school and home, and he was showing signs of depression. When I spoke with him, he told me, "I can't sleep, so I just stay up and play video games."

He was right about not sleeping, but he wasn't clued in about the root of the problem. Adam had a computer in his room. His parents caught him staying up several nights to play games and look at pornography.

When they confronted him, he argued, "Well, you don't know what it's like to not be able to sleep."

I hung out with Adam several times on youth-ministry camping trips and observed him without him realizing it. I know what sleep problems look like.

You see, I have severe sleep problems. I've had them ever since I was a kid. Numerous therapists have described me as ADHD and OCD among other things. Many wanted to prescribe various medications. Regardless, I didn't sleep well at night. I had a hard time shutting down my thoughts. I remember spending much of my childhood wandering around in the dark, exploring and getting into trouble.

Sleep never came easy to me.

I know the symptoms, the causes, and the countless theories about potential remedies.

When I became an adult, my insomnia came in handy in my youth-ministry job. I remember being in charge of a couple hundred high school kids sleeping in a gym at a weeklong event. I was literally always the last person in the room to fall asleep. Teenagers were always surprised when they tried to sneak out hours after bedtime and I was waiting for them by the door.

That week, I watched Adam engage in all kinds of healthy activities during the day (undoubtedly more physical activity than he experienced at home), eat a healthy dinner without caffeine-filled beverages, and then go to bed without a screen (we were out of cell range, so no one had screens).

It's funny how the self-diagnosed insomniac slept like a baby night after night.

I didn't know it at the time, but what I observed in Adam was almost textbook. Screens, diet, and physical activity all affect sleep, and consequently, all of these affect a teen's behaviors the following day.

This is exactly why I think this issue is so vital. Screens in the bedroom affect sleep, and sleep affects mental health—*big-time*.

## What Happens When Young People Lose Sleep?

Dr. Michelle Guerrero and her colleagues with the Healthy Active Living and Obesity Research Group in Canada studied more than four thousand eight- to eleven-year-olds. In the study, researchers examined how recreational screen time, sleep, and even physical activity affect the tendency of kids to act impulsively during the day.[15]

I found this study fascinating because of the link they found between screen time, sleep, and mental health, specifically young people's ability to finish tasks and their outbursts when things didn't go their way. Interestingly enough, two factors that influence impulsivity rose to the top in their findings: *sleep and screen time.*

When kids got more sleep (nine to eleven hours per night) and engaged in fewer than two hours a day of recreational screen time, they scored higher in eight out of eight domains of impulsivity. More sleep and less screen time equals fewer impulsive behaviors.

I think it's worth noting that physical activity is also a factor that affects sleep. When kids are more active during the day, they sleep better at night, plain and simple. Ask any youth worker who takes a group of kids skiing for the day. They all sleep like babies that night.

If kids are just sitting around all day watching Netflix or playing video games, then once again they aren't getting the exercise they need, which affects sleep. Screen time affects sleep in so many ways. So I wasn't surprised when these researchers found that sleep and screen time are the top two factors that influence kids' behaviors during the day.

The researchers concluded that limiting recreational screen time and promoting adequate sleep helps kids avoid impulsive decisions, and in turn, they will engage in less risky behaviors.

The research linking sleep and mental health is immeasurable. When your kids' sleep suffers, so does their mental health.

But it actually extends further than that. The consequences of poor sleep habits are numerous:

- *Poor school performance.* Kids who sleep less earn worse grades. Yes, it's almost as simple as that. The National Sleep Foundation examined a study that measured sleep and school performance in children and concluded that "one of the best predictors of school failure . . . [is] children's fatigue."[16]

- *Drowsy driving.* Research reveals that driving while tired is "comparable to driving with a blood alcohol content of .08 [percent], the legal limit of intoxication."[17]

- *Obesity.* Studies show that "for each hour of sleep lost, the odds of obesity increased [in adolescents] by 80%."[18]

- *Behavioral problems.* Almost every study on sleep connects poor sleep with negative behaviors. This ranges from being more vulnerable to drug and alcohol consumption to simply being impatient and grumpy. (Have you ever noticed in your own relationships that you tend to be short with people when you're tired?)

These consequences are significant, but let's look at the biggest consequence of sleep loss on kids: poor mental health.

## Your Kids' Mental Well-Being

A study by the University of Texas Health Science Center revealed that teens are four to five times more likely to be depressed if they are sleep deprived.[19]

Sleep deprivation and depression have a curious connection. I say *curious* because the relationship is a two-way street. Kids who are depressed definitely struggle with sleep, but kids who struggle with sleep also have a much higher chance of becoming depressed. The research showing a two-way relationship between poor sleep and poor mental health is undeniable.

In a Harvard Medical School article titled "Sleep and Mental Health," experts conclude that sleep deprivation can affect your mental health. A study they cite from a Michigan health maintenance organization found that, similar to the University of Texas study, adults who reported a history of insomnia were four times more likely to develop major depression within three years. Harvard researchers concluded,

> The brain basis of a mutual relationship between sleep
> and mental health is not yet completely understood. But
> neuroimaging and neurochemistry studies suggest that a good
> night's sleep helps foster both mental and emotional resilience,
> while chronic sleep deprivation sets the stage for negative
> thinking and emotional vulnerability.[20]

Don't forget the other study I cited earlier in this chapter, where researchers found that each hour of lost sleep resulted in a 38 percent increase in the "odds of [teens] feeling sad and hopeless" and a 58 percent increase in suicide attempts.[21]

The American Academy of Pediatrics concludes that "addressing insomnia will greatly improve treatment of depression."[22]

Any counselor will tell you that one of the first questions therapists ask patients who are struggling with depression is "How are you sleeping?"

Sleep is vital.

Screen time on social media is never a good trade-off.

## Create a Climate of Comfortable Conversation

So how can you talk with your kids about screens in the bedroom? Again, practice what you've learned in the last two chapters about creating a climate of comfortable conversation about these issues.

1. When you read something in this book that piques your interest, bring it up at a family gathering. Break the ice with a fun question. For example, "If you didn't have any rules telling you when you had to go to bed, and you could stay up as late as you wanted, what would you stay up doing, and what time do you think you'd finally go to bed?"

2. Bring up the issue you'd like to talk about by reading a note-worthy paragraph or study. Then ask your kids' opinions. Listen; don't lecture. Just ask questions, such as . . .

   • Why do you think sleep affects school performance, driving, obesity, and behavioral problems so much?

   • What are the biggest reasons you think phones keep kids awake at night?

   • Why do you think that about eight out of ten kids bring their phones into their bedrooms at night?

3. Practice empathy by stepping into your kids' shoes and trying to understand their viewpoints and feelings. Don't criticize their responses; just listen.

4. Ask your kids, "What do you think is best? How would you solve the problem at hand?" Or, in this case, ask, "So how do you think parents should respond when their kids want screens in the bedroom?"

5. Delay correction or decisions. Actually walk away. Don't rush to set boundaries or impose a decision right away. Tell your kids you need some time to think and pray about the situation.

You'll see these steps repeated over and over as you're reading this book. When you finish the book, add this step:

6. Set a time to talk about what you've read and make some decisions about screens. Give your kids advance notice. You might say, "This Thursday we're going out for pizza to talk about how we can become screenwise in this house."

And when that day comes, and you decide that phones will no longer be allowed in bedrooms, your kids will probably argue, "But I need my phone as an alarm clock."

That's when you'll just smile and say, "Well, there's another device that does that for you nicely. It's called *an alarm clock*! Here's twelve dollars. You can buy one at Target."

## Discussion Questions

1. What is the most compelling reason why kids shouldn't have phones in their bedrooms?

2. Why do you think there's such an undeniable link between sleep loss and depression?

3. Have you ever noticed your kids showing any of the consequences or symptoms of sleep loss we discussed in this chapter? What did you observe?

4. Why do you think some parents don't enforce the vital guideline "No screens in the bedroom"?

5. Do you think parents need to model this guideline by doing the same with their own phones? Why or why not?

6. What screen activity could be affecting your kids' sleep?

7. How can you create a climate of comfortable conversation about screens in the bedroom this week?

## CHAPTER 5

# The Unintended Effects of Social Media

*And how to build your kids' self-esteem*

I ALWAYS FIND IT INTRIGUING when researchers with opposing viewpoints actually agree on something. And one of the few things they came to a consensus about recently, with very little pushback, are the effects of social media on kids' mental health—*especially teenage girls.*

Social media is creating a pressurized environment for young people today, and their mental well-being is paying the price.

Why does social media impact mental health more than video games, music, or TV? And why more so since the release of smartphones?

Those are great questions. And the answers are becoming increasingly clear the more kids carry social media in their pockets.

Let's take a closer look at why too much social media is hurting your kids' mental health, what you can do to prevent it, and how you can be proactive about building your kids' self-esteem.

## The Barometer of Self-Esteem

I had a really tough time in middle school. I didn't have many friends, and I ate quite a few lunches alone. One particular kid had it out for me. He and his friends practiced everything in the bullying handbook: knocking my books off my desk, slapping the back of my neck on cold mornings, writing embarrassing insults across my locker in permanent marker. Those were difficult years.

Most of my friends didn't have it as tough as I did, but few of them would say those years were easy. It's probably fair to say that adolescents have always struggled with fitting in.

But back then we all had one saving grace—a break from the pressure to be liked. For me, the final bell rang at 2:42 p.m., and I sprinted home to where I was safe until 7:55 the next morning. More than seventeen hours away from the torment.

But kids today don't get a break from the pressure.

Now, at 2:42 p.m., the phones come out and kids enter a whole new world where they're compared not only to their peers at school but to kids all over the world—kids who are better looking and more creative, with more likes and followers. In fact, each of these attributes are problematically represented by a number that everyone on social media can see:

- Olivia, 843 friends. She just posted a picture of herself and two friends at the lake: 327 likes.
- Tyler, 1,043 friends. He just posted a picture of his new truck: 278 likes.
- Isabella, 962 friends. She just posted a picture of her new shoes: 246 likes.

These are the elite kids.

Then there are the normal kids like Katherine. She's fun, creative, sweet . . . and on the swim team. But she has *only* 237 friends—a number that pales in comparison to the elite kids. And her last picture of her dog, Pugsly, wearing a sweater earned a mere 43 likes.

Do you think Katherine noticed?

*Absolutely.*

The numbers stare her in the face every time she opens up her social media profile. And scrolling down doesn't help. More of the same.

- Lily, with her long hair, perfect teeth, and 629 friends, posted a picture of her cat yawning: 159 likes.

- Chloe, tan and beautiful, with 864 friends, posted a picture of her checkered Vans: 184 likes.

- Logan, a lacrosse player with 1,385 friends, posted a picture of himself and his girlfriend, Mia, before homecoming: 383 likes.

The pressure is on.

*Followers.*

*Likes.*

I'm sure Steve Jobs never intended it, but the smartphone has become a real-time, portable barometer of self-esteem. It not only tells kids exactly how popular they are and how well liked their posts are; it also exposes them to a nonstop panel of cowardly critics who comment on their posts from the safety of their anonymous usernames.

> *The smartphone has become a real-time, portable barometer of self-esteem.*

Fitting in has never been so difficult.

## A Consensus

So is all this pressure taking a toll on our kids' mental health?

The debate has been ongoing for almost a decade.

Are smartphones bad for kids?

Is the increase of screen time linked to the unprecedented rise in depression, anxiety, and teen suicide?

Before I answer these questions, I should note that we're not talking about a small increase. One in five adolescent girls experienced a major depressive episode at some point during 2017.[1] That's an 84 percent increase during the past decade. And a report from the US Department of Health and Human Services (HHS) revealed that suicide rates among Americans ages ten to twenty-four increased by 56 percent between 2007 and 2017.[2] The iPhone came out in 2007. The biggest increases occurred among the very young, with suicide rates nearly tripling during that time period in ten- to fourteen-year-olds.

Researchers have been scratching their heads looking for the cause. Many have seen a correlation between suicide rates among teens and the increase in screen time that smartphones have created. Dr. Jean Twenge points this out in her article "Stop Debating Whether Too Much Smartphone Time Can Hurt Teens, and Start Protecting Them." She says,

> Four large studies of teens from the U.S. and U.K. all show the same thing: happiness and mental health are the highest at a half-hour to two hours of extracurricular digital media use a day; well-being then steadily decreases, with those who spend the most time online being the worst off.[3]

But here's where the debate gets interesting. With researchers still disagreeing, Jonathan Haidt created an open-source literature review, pasting in the abstracts of all relevant studies he could find on both sides of the issue. He invited other researchers to add to the document, hoping to reach a consensus as to whether social media is a contributing factor in the increased rates of depression, anxiety, self-harm, and suicide among adolescents.[4]

In 2020, while I was writing this book, all of these researchers came to a consensus, basically agreeing on two undeniable truths:

1. A mental-health crisis is indeed consuming adolescents, particularly girls, in all of the major English-speaking countries.

2. When the data for both genders are combined, the evidence linking screen time to these mental-health problems is weak and inconsistent. But when you limit the analysis to the effects of social media on girls, the link is strong and consistent.

What does this mean?

In short, these researchers overwhelmingly agreed that our girls are paying a price when they spend too much time on social media.

But these conclusions certainly aren't unanimous. I just read a report today in which researchers claim that the amount of time adolescents spend on social media is *not* reliably linked to serious mental-health problems, such as depression and anxiety. They insist there simply isn't enough evidence. I can't help but wonder if this particular group of researchers has ever actually hung out with kids, because almost every youth worker I know clearly observes this link—specifically when girls spend too much time on social media. (We'll talk more about this in the next chapter on screen time.)

Even though most experts have

*Researchers overwhelmingly agree that our girls are paying a price when they spend too much time on social media.*

71

observed that young people suffer mental-health problems when they spend too much time on screens, it would be a mistake to lump all screen time together and call it evil. Netflix and Spotify, for example, don't appear to have an observable negative impact on our kids' mental health. But when we look into that social media app our kids love so much, *Houston, we have a problem.*

Researchers also agreed that the *more time* adolescents, especially girls, spend on social media, the stronger the connection is to mental-health problems. There is actually little evidence of harm for light daily usage (one hour a day). But most researchers observed harmful effects with heavy social media use (two or more hours per day).

Some studies even revealed that the rate of depression doubles as kids move from light to heavy social media use.[5] In the same way, in seven out of eight studies, researchers observed an improvement in some measures of mental health or happiness after reducing or eliminating social media use for a few weeks.[6]

Bottom line: not only does social media affect the mental health of our kids, especially girls, but the number of hours they spend on social media each day makes a difference.

The most recent studies tracking exactly how many hours young people spend on screens is eye opening, because social media takes up a good chunk of it. Eight- to twelve-year-olds average one hour and seventeen minutes a day on social media sites like Instagram and Snapchat.[7] But if you add in the amount of time they also watch online videos on apps like YouTube, which are technically also social media, the numbers go way up. (And this category of online videos doesn't include TV shows on apps like Netflix, which is yet another category.) Eight- to twelve-year-olds average an additional hour and forty-four minutes daily watching online videos, which are often funny clips from influencers.[8] Here's the breakdown showing how much time eight- to twelve-year-olds spend on social media:

Social media . . . . . . . . . . . . . . . . . 1 hour 17 minutes per day

Online videos (not TV) . . . . . . . . . . . 1 hour 44 minutes per day

TOTAL SOCIAL MEDIA . . . . . . . . . . . 3 hours and 1 minute per day

Recommended time: . . . . . . . . . . . . No more than 1 or 2 hours per day

Teenagers from thirteen to eighteen years of age spend even more time on social media: an average of one hour and fifty-six minutes per day. But they also spend an average of an additional hour and thirty-seven minutes per day watching online videos, with YouTube as their app of choice.[9] Here's the breakdown for this age group:

Social media . . . . . . . . . . . . . . . . . 1 hour 56 minutes per day

Online videos (not TV) . . . . . . . . . . . 1 hour 37 minutes per day

TOTAL SOCIAL MEDIA . . . . . . . . . . . 3 hours 33 minutes per day

Recommended time: . . . . . . . . . . . . No more than 1 or 2 hours per day

You might think, *What's the big deal with these online videos?*

That's exactly what teens say. Yet online videos are one of the biggest reasons young people overwhelmingly want to become online influencers in some shape or form.

## Follow Me

Ethan is sixteen years old and spends every spare moment making gaming videos and posting them to his YouTube channel. He already has more than four thousand followers. His dream is to get sponsored and become a full-time influencer.

Ethan isn't alone. He is among 86 percent of kids in Generation Z who want to become social media influencers.[10] Eighty percent of thirteen- to eighteen-year-olds want to be self-employed in the future, 73 percent as freelancers.[11] Ethan has already dropped the bomb on his parents that he doesn't want to go to college. He wants to create gaming videos as a full-time gig.

Ethan has always loved gaming, and he's good at it—so good that all of his friends watch him to learn how to pass certain levels in new games. He purchases new games on the release date as if it's a career and plays them nonstop, except while attending school, eating meals, and catching a little sleep. Within a week, he's an expert on a particular game, posting reviews and chiming in on strategy in popular gaming forums.

But Ethan needs more followers.

Every influencer does.

Back when Ethan was fourteen, one of his friends filmed him cracking jokes while conquering a new *Call of Duty* game and posted it to YouTube. The video tallied more than fifty thousand views the first week. That's when Ethan got the idea to become an influencer.

A lot of young people post videos of themselves gaming, but Ethan's combination of humor and skill made him pretty popular.

Problem is, followers are a lot harder to come by than Ethan fathomed. He figured that fifty thousand views should generate fifty thousand followers. But Ethan soon realized that viewers might watch ten seconds and then move on to another video, then another and another and another. Getting a viewer to stay a couple of minutes and then subscribe to his YouTube channel is a whole 'nother feat—one that began keeping Ethan awake at night.

*Why does this guy JoshMerc have 123,000 followers when he's so lame!* Ethan wondered.

That's one of the things that happens with social media: *comparisons.*

It's inevitable in the social media world, regardless of the platform. If you want to be a YouTube star, there's always someone with more followers (unless your name is PewDiePie).

That's one of the by-products of kids "just watching videos" on

YouTube or TikTok. Many kids see new "role models" posting fun videos and think, *I could do that.*

In fact, whenever I talk about the subject of kids wanting to be influencers, I'm always overwhelmed with how many parents come up to me after a workshop and talk about one of their kids who spends every waking moment on YouTube and wants to be the next Dude Perfect.

My friend Julie teaches third grade, and every week she interviews one of her students in front of the class, asking questions like "What do you want to be when you grow up?" She said that years ago, kids always responded, "A doctor," "a dolphin trainer," or "president of the United States." Now, she says, eight out of ten students say, "I want to be a YouTuber."

There's similar pressure on Instagram to be an Insta-celeb. Your kids' generation has grown up seeing nobodies become somebodies on Instagram doing simple things like putting on makeup or posting funny pics. And they think, *I could do that.*

Dealing with our kids' aspirations is a difficult position for parents, because we don't want to be dream crushers. But at the same time, we don't want our kids tossing away college plans to aim for Insta-celebridom (I think I just made up that word). More importantly, we don't want our kids to put themselves at risk physically and emotionally in an attempt to be influencers. I've seen kids do both far too many times.

The physical harm lies in the simple fact that kids become willing to do almost *anything* to get more followers, including engaging in risky behaviors. Kids sometimes try stupid stunts. For instance, consider the Fire Challenge, where kids try to light themselves on fire and post the video on YouTube (no, I'm not making this up).[12]

Let me be clear: stunts like these, including the choking game and the Tide Pod Challenge, are real, but they aren't commonplace. The everyday risk that most kids take today is simply leaving their profiles on the public setting, which allows anyone to follow them. This is so common in a culture where kids want followers at any cost that I'm devoting an entire chapter to it (chapter 7, "I See You").

In fact, some social media profiles now even default to "public" when your kids download the app and sign in the first time. I recently reviewed a social media app that gave this warning to kids if they flipped the switch to private: "Are you sure you want to do this? By switching to private, your potential followers won't be able to follow you without sending you a request."

Here's the main point: if your kids keep their profiles public, pedophiles will surely find them, look at their pictures undetected, and in most cases, discover more information about your kids than they ever intended to reveal.

The pressure to get more followers is also taking an emotional toll on our kids, which is probably one of the biggest reasons all of those researchers reached the consensus that too much social media is harmful. All the pressure to be liked and followed is stressing our kids out.

Consider Sam Benarroch, who had about 166,000 followers on social media but purposely took a break from it because of the anxiety he experienced when his "likes" started dropping. Sam confessed,

> Not getting the numbers that you want is so harmful. . . .
> It's scary because it's this spiral of not ever feeling like you're
> enough, and that leaves this mental scarring. It's contributed to
> my mental health not being the best lately. I definitely had to
> get some therapy because of this.[13]

So how can we help steer our kids away from spending too much time on social media?

## Five Ways to Protect Your Kids from the Dangers of Social Media

### 1. Delay Social Media.

If your kids ask for social media before they're thirteen years of age, the simple answer you can give them is, "I'm sorry. It's against the law."

As I mentioned in chapter 3, the Federal Trade Commission (FTC) prohibits websites and social media apps, including Snapchat, Instagram, TikTok, and Twitter, from collecting personal information from kids under thirteen without parental consent.

### 2. Discuss the Dangers of Social Media.

When your kids turn thirteen and ask, "Mom, can I download TikTok?" it's time to talk with them about the dangers. At the beginning of this book, I pointed out that most parents would never throw their kids the car keys without first making sure they know how to drive responsibly. If they want to drive, kids have to wait until they're the correct age. Then they're required to take a driver's education course, pass a written test, and even take a road test.

Isn't it bizarre how hands-off our society has been about educating our kids to use social media responsibly?

Think about it. Even with anxiety, depression, and suicide at unprecedented levels, and countless warnings from the mental-health community about smartphones and social media, most parents still just hand their kids a phone with very little instruction. In fact, I find that most parents say, "My kids know more about this device than I do."

I think moms and dads need to rethink this. Even though kids might be more tech savvy, they certainly aren't *wiser* about what to post, whom to friend, what to stream, or how much screen time might be too much.

This is why I always encourage parents to set the parental controls on their kids' devices so they can't add an app without Mom's or Dad's pass code. This prompts kids to ask Mom or Dad, "Can I download this new app?" This is especially important for the first few years they have a phone.

When your kids ask you this question, it's always best to respond, "I don't know. Let's check it out together."

This simple response doesn't just give your kids a yes or no. It opens the door for dialogue. It gives you an opportunity to sit down with them and teach them how to look at any app objectively and evaluate its content.

So let's say one of your kids asks to download a new social media app called Friendmigo (yes, I just made that up).

"Mom, can I have Friendmigo?"

You reply, "I don't know. Let's check it out together."

Then sit down on the couch with your laptop and start by googling "Friendmigo safety," and then maybe "Friendmigo parental concerns." You'll typically find several articles. Read about the app together, then discuss these questions with your child:

- Does the site publicly display how many followers or friends users have? Does it count likes? This factor alone shouldn't rule out an app. Many innocent social media sites have these features, but they can also create a pressurized environment where young people compare themselves with other users.

- Does the site encourage anonymity, where kids can hide behind a screen name or an avatar and be whoever they want to be? Anonymity removes accountability and gives some users the idea that they can say or do whatever they want, with no consequences. These sites might claim they allow kids to express themselves "honestly," but typically they're full of bullying, violent threats, sexual content, and foul language.

- Does the site offer ephemeral posting, where pictures or messages are visible for a short time and then disappear? This feature can breed irresponsibility, because kids feel like there is no record to their online activity.

- Does the site encourage meeting strangers? Sites like these are popular but very dangerous, especially when they connect people based on geographic proximity—"Hey, cool, this guy I met in our town named Ted Bundy wants to meet me tonight."

- Does the site encourage hookups, where people connect with each other only for sexual purposes? Some dating sites might brag about being "a fun way to connect with new and interesting people," when they're really just hookup sites.

- Does the app effectively monitor and filter inappropriate content?

- Does the app reveal your location, and can you turn off this feature? Kids should never give strangers their location.

- Does the website offer any age verification? I almost hesitated writing this because social media rarely verifies age anymore. But it's important for kids to realize that followers can be whatever age they want to be online.

- What do other website reviews say about this social media app? Has Plugged In reviewed it? Has Common Sense Media written about it? If several sites warn you about common problems, pay attention.

- What rating are other review sites giving this social media app? Are they calling it appropriate for kids? Or do they say, "We recommend this for ages fifteen and up"?

You'll probably find that at least one or two of these questions will red-flag most social media apps, and you'll have to make a discerning decision. For example, Instagram currently shows how many followers and likes users have, but it's pretty good at monitoring content and doesn't celebrate anonymity. Instagram can be a pretty innocent place for young people to post fun pics, but it can also put a lot of pressure on them—especially girls—to get more likes and followers.

You'll need to weigh these elements as you evaluate each app with your kids.

So engage your kids in conversations about these issues. Teach them to recognize some of the dangers of social media. This could be as simple as grabbing my *Teen's Guide to Social Media* book and telling your kids, "This book is your new phone contract. Meet with me each week, and we'll discuss a chapter at a time. When you finish the book, you can have Instagram."

## 3. Limit Social Media.

Once your kids get on social media, take the advice of researchers and limit their screen time. Don't let your kids average two hours a day scrolling through their social media profiles, and another two hours a day watching online videos that make them feel the desire (dare I say the pressure) to become influencers themselves.

I'll be honest, this step is by far the most difficult for parents. Some apps have individual limits. As I write this, TikTok enables parents to set controls limiting the app to just forty minutes a day. But kids are smart. Sometimes they'll open a second app and sign up under a second username or on a second device and use a different profile without limits. (That old phone you forgot about in a drawer, or that old iTouch your kids used to have can both download apps and run on Wi-Fi.)

This is why boundaries are not as effective as bonding. In other words, discussing the dangers of social media with your kids is far more important than limiting social media. That doesn't mean you shouldn't limit it. But as I said earlier, *rules won't raise your kids*. You need to teach them how to make discerning decisions on their own.

One of the best ways to limit social media is by adhering to what you learned in chapter 4: keep your kids' devices out of their bedrooms at night. These practices and other family media habits, such as "No tech at the table" and watching media together as a family, keep kids from isolating in their bedrooms for hours at a time, sometimes at unhealthy levels. (We'll talk a little more about this in the next chapter about screen time.)

You could also follow the steps you learned about in chapter 2:

- Set up a family gathering.

- Bring up a topic and ask your kids' opinions about it.

- Practice empathy by stepping into their shoes and listening to their viewpoints and feelings.

- Ask your kids what they think is best and how they would solve the problem.

- Delay correction and decisions. Actually walk away. Let your kids know you need time to think and pray about your decision.

- When you finish this book, set a time for your family to talk about what you read and decide what social media limits are fair and helpful.

### 4. Seek Out Fun Tech-Free Activities.

I just suggested limiting social media. As parents, we sometimes find ourselves getting so caught up in telling our kids what *not* to do that we forget to teach them what *to* do. So if you find yourself constantly saying, "Hey, get off YouTube" or "How much social media is that today?" try to shift the focus to affirming positive activities and being proactive about doing nonscreen activities together.

During the global COVID pandemic, many families were stuck together, experiencing screen overload with nowhere else to go. So they became creative, building a firepit in the backyard and roasting s'mores, working on puzzles together, or even taking family walks or hikes.

Sometimes the simplest activities can bring families together.

In my house, whenever my wife began making cookie dough, she would literally announce, "I'm making cookie dough!" It was funny how the kids all began popping their heads out of their rooms like prairie dogs—well, horizontal prairie dogs. Within five minutes, the whole family was gathered around the bowl sneaking handfuls of cookie dough. (Yes, we risked getting salmonella in our house.) But guess what? Whenever kids had cookie dough all over their hands, their phones were nowhere to be seen. In our house, cookie dough meant laughing, talking, and stuffing our faces with unhealthy goodness.

What are some simple tech-free activities your kids would enjoy? How can you be proactive about initiating a few of these activities this week?

### 5. Remind Your Kids of Their Identity.

Another vital practice that's probably the most effective at helping your kids see the dangers of social media is to remind them of who they truly are. It's funny, but sometimes the best defense is a good offense.

I stated an important principle in step 4, and I'm going to state it again: as parents, sometimes we find ourselves getting so caught up in telling our kids what *not* to do that we forget to teach them what *to* do.

In the same way, we can get so caught up trying to warn our kids about bad influences that we never encourage them to follow good influences. The world is full of confusing messages about who we are. Make sure your kids are hearing the truth about their identity. Because whenever we give Christ control of our lives, our old identity is gone, and we have a new identity (2 Corinthians 5:17).

Have you talked to your kids about their identity in Christ? Wouldn't it be cool if kids understood not only how valuable they are to God but also who they are in Christ?

If your kids have put their faith in Jesus, they don't have to get caught up in "self." That's the world's thinking. In actuality, self has been "crucified with Christ. It is no longer I who live, but Christ who lives in me" (Galatians 2:20).

Interestingly enough, when kids spend excessive time plugged into entertainment media, they'll hear plenty of distracting messages about who they are or where happiness comes from: popularity, good looks, instant gratification. The best way to counter these lies is to be proactive about teaching your kids biblical truth.

Consider Colossians 3:2-3: "Think about the things of heaven, not the things of earth. For you died to this life, and your real life is hidden with Christ in God" (NLT).

Sure, you can buy devotionals with all kinds of good discussion guides to help your kids understand their identity in Christ. But don't be afraid to just open the Bible as well.

For example, take a few verses from Psalm 119:

Blessed are those whose way is blameless,
 who walk in the law of the LORD!
Blessed are those who keep his testimonies,
 who seek him with their whole heart,
who also do no wrong,
 but walk in his ways! (119:1-3)

Read these verses aloud and then ask your kids questions about what you read, such as . . .

- What does *blameless* mean?
- What does that look like today?
- What does it mean to walk in the law of the Lord?
- How can we get to know the law of the Lord better?
- What does that look like today?
- Why does it say to "keep" God's testimonies and not just "do" them once? What's the difference?

I've downloaded some excellent free Bible apps, including the Blue Letter Bible, where you can click on any verse, look up the words in the original language, and even see what scholars like David Guzik have to say about them. These resources can be really helpful if you're trying to start a discussion with your kids.

The more we dialogue with our kids about God's truth, the more they'll recognize Satan's and the world's lies. And this world is full of lies about who your kids are or who they should try to be.

One of the most effective ways I've found to help kids engage in meaningful conversations about their identity is through music. Young people love music, and many songs today stir up feelings about self. We can use these songs to point them to God's Word.

Step back to 2018 and think of the popular Lauren Daigle song "You Say." In the song, she talks about the voices we hear in our heads that say "You're not enough" and the lies that tell us we'll never measure up.[14]

Songs like this one are great to play for your kids and then talk about. Simply ask your kids, "Do you ever feel like this?"

The Christian band For King & Country has a powerful music video for the song "God Only Knows." Jump on YouTube and watch that video with your kids. Then ask them these questions:

- What stands out to you as you watch this video?
- Do you know anyone who feels like this girl?
- Have you ever felt like this girl? How so?
- How did the friend in the video reach out to her friend at the end?
- Do you have someone like that in your life?

Are you engaging your kids in conversations that give them a chance to explore the love God has for them?

In 2020 I had the opportunity to lead a group of families in my neighborhood through a study of Jesus' words in the Beatitudes from His Sermon on the Mount. This powerful little passage is packed with perspective. (Do you like my use of alliteration?) In a world where so many people are caught up in money, looks, and status, this passage walks us through the things that really matter. Most importantly, it reminds us that we have all we need every day just by putting our faith in Jesus and being part of His Kingdom.

I led this study much as I did in the earlier example from Psalm 119. I read a verse and then broke it down. So first I read "Blessed are the poor in spirit" (Matthew 5:3).

The word *blessed* here basically means "joy because God has given you everything you need." You don't need anything the world provides. How could this kind of joy change your perspective?

*Poor in spirit* means to realize your own shortcomings and be utterly dependent on God. It's complete humility before God. Why does realizing our need for Him give us a joy beyond comprehension?

This passage is eye opening.

When I did this study, I rarely had to argue that social media is harmful and entertainment is twisted. Instead, I just opened up the truth of God's Word, and the young people there soaked it in.

Martin Luther King Jr. said, "Darkness cannot drive out darkness; only light can do that."

Are you having these conversations with your kids?

## Discussion Questions

1. What are some of the fun aspects of social media?

2. What are some of the dangers you notice?

3. Why do you think research shows that social media seems to negatively affect girls more than boys?

4. Why does social media affect girls this way more than gaming or watching Netflix?

5. Let's say your kid asks for permission to download an app, and you respond, "I don't know. Let's check it out together." What resources would you access to begin discussing the app?

6. What are some of the practical ways you can try to limit your kids' social media use to a healthy one or two hours a day max?

7. How can you engage your kids in conversations about their identity in Christ this week?

## CHAPTER 6

# The Thing about Screen Time

*Helping your kids learn to make wise screen-time choices*

NATALIE IS FOURTEEN YEARS OLD, and like most of her friends, she's had her smartphone since middle school. But after a few huge blowups over how much time she was "wasting" on her phone, her parents limited her screen time to just two hours a day. It was "unfair and oppressive" in Natalie's opinion, but her mom had read some article about it.

*So it was written; so it shall be done.*

Natalie's parents don't really know what Natalie is doing on her phone. The reality is that social media is the one screen activity that seems to draw her in and distract her from what's important.

Natalie's app of choice is TikTok. She has Instagram and a few others as well, but TikTok is the one that distracts her from her homework. Whenever she opens up the app, she loses track of time. That's what happens on TikTok. Kids are watching a never-ending variety show of the most popular acts in the world. The app quickly discovers what they like to watch and provides them with an endless supply of it, in unedited form.

Natalie's parents never look at the app, so they have no idea what their daughter is watching. But they do occasionally remind her, "Only two hours, right?"

"Yes, Mom. I probably don't even hit that anymore," Natalie insists.

She isn't really intending to lie, but she's clocking *way* over that.

She's not alone. The average teenager clocks more then seven hours of screen time daily.[1] These numbers vary by age, gender, and other factors—even household income. For example, teens from higher-income homes ($100,000 or more) average six hours and forty-nine minutes per day of daily screen time, while teens from lower-income homes (less than $35,000) average eight hours and thirty-two minutes per day.[2]

This is just screen time. It doesn't even include the time kids spend listening to music on Spotify or iTunes. That's a lot of entertainment media.

Natalie is a good student and an athlete, so she doesn't quite approach the seven-hour average, but she easily doubles her screen-time limit, exceeding two hours on social media alone.

Her attachment to her phone is evident seconds after her phone alarm goes off in the morning. *Her phone is right by her bedside.*

The first thing she does after turning off her alarm is check Instagram. In middle school, all of her friends used Snapchat, but now Instagram is Natalie's main way of connection with her friends.

Typically she'll check a few of her friends' stories, along with a couple of celebs she follows. Then on the way to school, she'll scroll through her Insta-feed to see who's doing what. Once she's caught up, she'll open TikTok until she arrives at the campus.

Then she'll greet her friends, but before school, everyone's phones are still out. Sometimes she and her friends will show each other a funny post or video they saw the night before. Then they'll all return texts and DMs.

By the time the first bell rings, it's unusual if Natalie has spent less than thirty minutes on her phone.

Phones are supposed to be kept in students' pockets during the school day, unless a teacher specifically allows students to have them out. Two of Natalie's teachers don't mind students pulling out their phones when their work is finished. And kids tend to find other times to use their phones, such as in the bathrooms or in between classes when no adults are around. Natalie can usually clock in another twenty to thirty minutes of screen time during school. And honestly, that's a lot less than most of her friends.

Natalie clocks another ten minutes close to or during soccer practice. And another ten on the way home.

By the time Natalie arrives home, she's usually approaching ninety minutes of screen time.

Before dinner, Natalie showers and then plops on her bed and looks at TikTok videos, thinking, *I bet I could do that.* She doesn't want to become a full-time influencer by any means. But it would be fun to have enough followers to get a few sponsors.

No screens are allowed during dinnertime at Natalie's house. But dinner is usually only about fifteen minutes, and then everybody scatters. That's when Natalie attacks her homework—with her phone right next to her books.

And that's where screen time is pretty hard to track:

Do math three minutes uninterrupted.

*Bzzzzzzz.*

*Who's that? Oh. Just Kristen posting a picture of her stupid Frenchie.*

Math one minute.

*Bzzzzzzz.*

*Michael trying to flirt.*

Math two minutes.

*Bzzzzzzz.*

*Alexis posting a rant about an unfair quiz Mr. Reynolds gave. Tons of kids are commenting. Ha. Chris Mangold is so funny.*

Math one minute.

*Bzzzzzzz.*

*Michael again. Another DM talking about a video, and a link.*

Natalie watches the four-minute video. *Some girl from Atlanta posted it. She's a really good dancer.* Then Natalie swipes to see some of her other videos. *They're good.* She clocks another twenty minutes watching her videos.

Natalie's mom peeks in the door and sees Natalie looking at her phone.

"Natalie, aren't you supposed to be doing homework?"

"I am," Natalie says, throwing her phone aside and picking up her pencil. "I just need my phone for my homework. Group project."

"Well, don't get distracted," her mom says. "Remember your two-hour limit."

"I'm not distracted, Mom. I've barely been on my phone at all today. I haven't had time."

Natalie knows she's stretching the truth a bit. But honestly, she has no idea that she's already spent more than two hours on social media alone. And when she finishes her homework, she'll clock in at least an hour on Netflix and another hour on social media, depending on the night. And once her lights are out, she often scrolls through social media in her bed until she falls asleep. This can last twenty minutes . . . *or hours.*

After all is said and done, Natalie typically spends about four to six hours on her screen each day, well short of the average screen time for teens her age.

Is this too much?

Should Natalie's parents do anything different?

## How Much Time?

Nearly every expert agrees it's wise for moms and dads to set some helpful screen-time limits for their kids. The question is, how much?

Wouldn't it be nice if the answer was a simple number?

*Two hours of screen time. No more.*

And how do you track something so sprinkled throughout the day?

Sadly, it's not that simple. On top of that, all screen time is not created equal. I think America witnessed this in 2020 during the COVID-19 outbreak, when everyone was sequestered in their homes. No contact with anyone—*except through screens.* Even those who were set against screen use realized that if they prohibited screens, they were cutting off their kids' distance learning and social connection. All screen time is not the same.

It makes sense. Your daughter's Zoom call to her cousin shouldn't be lumped in the same category as scrolling through her Instagram feed. We're talking about two very different screen activities. In fact, most experts would actually *recommend* using screens to engage in conversations with extended family. And yes, as we read in the previous chapter, most experts would severely caution against any young girl spending more than two hours a day on social media.

Screen time varies.

My nephew loves YouTube. Sometimes he's just watching silly videos. But at other times, he's learning new skills by watching talented guitar players. (He's getting really good.) His dad doesn't want to limit his guitar-learning YouTube time. But endless silly videos? And they're both on YouTube. How do you set parental controls for that?

How are parents expected to navigate this? And should they even worry about screen activities like playing video games or watching videos?

Honestly . . . is it too much work to track?

The good news is, doctors do almost unanimously agree on screen-time limits for young children. The research is pretty clear. As for adolescents, there is still some debate, but as you read in the last chapter, researchers from opposing viewpoints recently came to a consensus that too much social media has a negative effect on the mental health of our kids.

Let's look at some helpful screen-time recommendations; then I'll offer a few tips on how to apply them in your home.

## Screen Limits for Young Kids: Birth to Age Five

Screen-time recommendations are pretty clear for young kids. It's as simple as this:

- There should be no screen time for kids under two years of age.

- For kids two to five years old, limit screen time to just one or two hours a day of high-quality programming. (The American Academy of Pediatrics actually recommends only one hour per day.[3])

I know, I know. If I had kids under five years of age, I'd probably be screaming at this book right now: "Do you realize how hard it is to raise a two-year-old and a four-year-old?"

It's okay. Scream at me. I can take it. (I can't, actually. I'm kind of a wimp. *Way* too sensitive. But I don't mind if you yell at my book.)

When my three kids were one, three, and five years old, I watched them in the morning while my wife, Lori, was at work. And on many mornings by ten o'clock, I was already spent! (I told you I'm a wimp.) But I knew if I put on the movie *Aladdin* (one of my son's favorites), I had one hour and twenty-six minutes of peace and quiet (that's when the credits start to roll). Even my one-year-old would sit there in her baby bouncer and become entranced by the screen. (I'm admitting it.

I put my baby in front of a screen.) I'll be completely candid: It was wonderful! I cherished that ninety minutes.

Nothing held my kids' attention like *Aladdin*!

And now I hear parents tell me similar stories.

"If I don't give my kid my phone in the car, he freaks out!"

"If I limit my son's video-game time, he's a monster!"

I don't want to be the bad guy, and I don't want to go on a tangent about coddling or even enabling your kids, but I will say this: Don't get your kids hooked on screens early. An hour or two max.

You are the parent. It's okay to say no.

Let me add that most of the screen-demanding behaviors of kids are taught, not inherited. In other words, if we didn't give our kids our phones in the car in the first place, they wouldn't get in the habit of watching videos in the car, and we wouldn't have to deal with any tantrums when we suddenly deny them of that privilege.

Don't shoot the messenger. The fact is, the American Academy of Pediatrics has been recommending strict screen limits for years, and they've done the research to back it up.[4] Face-to-face connection with infants and toddlers is far superior. And if you do allow your two- to five-year-olds to watch any programming, experts recommend you watch it with them so you can dialogue with them about it and help them apply it to real life.

"Do you see what Sarah Connor is doing? She's training her son to evade the evil Terminator so he can save the human race. You can do the same with bullies at preschool." (Okay, maybe not that movie.)

So don't just plop your kids in front of the TV and take a nap. Watch their favorite show with them, and when you're done, play with them! Run up to your toddler and in your best Grover voice say, "Near." Tickle them, then run away and say, "Far."

Interacting with our kids is crucial. Most studies reveal that "passive screen time shouldn't replace reading, playing or problem-solving."[5]

In short, keep screens off as often as possible when your kids are young, especially in the evening hours. Research shows that "even infants exposed to screen media in the evening hours show significantly shorter night-time sleep duration than those with no evening screen exposure."[6]

A screen might seem like a great babysitter because TV makes your kids happy for the moment. But so do cake and ice cream for breakfast.

So be proactive about creating safe areas where kids can have unstructured play. Get toys that allow them to be creative and active. And mix in structured activities where you can interact with them about what you're doing. Take them on walks and talk about what you see around you. Bring them to a park or playground where they can play with other kids their age. And if your location permits, make a safe place in the yard where your kids can play outside.

I remember when my five-year-old would become restless and give me that "There's nothing to do" look. That's when I'd usually say, "Okay, time to go outside."

He would put on his little rubber boots, go into the backyard, and play. He was always a little pouty at first, but typically within about three to five minutes, I'd see him walking around with a stick, stabbing imaginary dragons, and making a fortress out of old boxes and lawn chairs.

And if I was being a really good parent, I would go out there with him after a while and say, "Can I play too?"

Yes, this takes a little more work.

Good parenting always does.

## Screen Limits for Preadolescents: Ages Six to Eleven

Here's where the limits on screen time become a little blurry. As kids grow and mature, you'll start to hear researchers who study the effects of screens on children say things like "Not all kids are the same" and "There is no one-size-fits-all approach."

But I find it interesting to note the areas where most researchers agree.

Studies vary in their conclusions about how much video-game time is too much or how much TV our kids should watch. But almost every study about preadolescents and screens agrees on the following guidelines:

- Don't allow social media for kids under thirteen. Yes, even though some app developers have created special social media apps for kids under thirteen, don't let your kids use them. (If you're wondering why, I encourage you to reread the previous chapter.)

- Set parental controls so kids can't download apps or access the web without Mom or Dad entering a password.

- Turn off the chat or live-play feature for video games that allows kids to connect with other people online. Your eight- or ten-year-old doesn't need to be chatting with a stranger on his or her gaming system. (In the next chapter, we'll talk about teaching kids how to recognize predatory behaviors. But don't put your preadolescent kids in a position where they have to do this.) Even if you control whom your kids connect with, you can't control whom those "friends" allow to play with them. If little Christopher is only allowed to connect with his cousin, but his cousin is allowed to connect with anyone online, then Christopher will be exposed to everyone his cousin lets into the "room."

- Turn off screens and put them away during meals. Yes, Mom and Dad, too.

- Create no-tech zones, such as bedrooms and the dinner table.

- Avoid screens one hour before bedtime. (Reread chapter 4 if you want to know why.)

- Turn off televisions when they're not in use. Yes, even the news.

- Avoid using media to calm your kids down.

- Make sure your kids are close by when they're watching screens, not off in a bedroom by themselves.

- Ask your kids regularly about what they're watching and what games or apps they're playing with. Dialogue about what they're seeing.

- Watch programming with your children and talk about what you see, especially advertising. Use these conversations as opportunities to educate your kids about the ads they're watching.

Yes, none of these guidelines talk about *how many hours*. That's because no one agrees on a specific "healthy" number of screen-time hours for preadolescents. But I think you'll find that if you adhere to the recommendations that experts *do* agree on, it really won't allow for a lot of screen time.

For example, consider the guideline "Make sure your kids are close by when they're watching screens, not off in a bedroom by themselves." This guideline alone will really help filter both the quality and quantity of screen time. If little eight-year-old Madison is flipping through the channels and lands on *Pulp Fiction*, Mom will hear Samuel L. Jackson yelling and switch channels.

That's one of the reasons I didn't allow headphones in my house. I wanted to hear what my kids were listening to. In fact, as they got older, I bought each of them a nice speaker for their phones so they could play loud music in their bedrooms.

Some of my friends asked me, "Jonathan, why did you get your kids big ol' speakers? Won't you constantly have to ask them to turn their music down?"

I always replied, "Because I considered the alternative: them listening to *who knows what* through headphones. Speakers provided a certain accountability while they were young."

For those of you who are still wondering, "Jonathan, if experts don't agree on specific screen-time limits, how many hours should I let my ten-year-old lie on the couch playing video games?"

Personally, I think that gaming screen time for this age group should be limited to just one or two hours a day, depending on the kid and his or her age. And I might make exceptions; for example, when Mom or Dad plays with their preadolescent kids.

Some kids don't even like video games and would rather sit and watch TV all day. Those kids might need TV screen-time limits. I say *need* because if we don't limit screen time, we'll start to see the consequences. For example, according to the Mayo Clinic, "too much or poor quality screen time" is associated with the following:

- obesity
- irregular sleep schedules and shorter duration of sleep
- behavioral problems
- loss of social skills
- violence
- less time for play[7]

This means you'll need to find some helpful screen limits that fit each of your kids in your setting. During the summer, you might let your kids have a little extra recreational screen time. If your nine-year-old is creative and loves to make little videos, you might not want to limit that screen time as much. But as soon as he wants to start posting those videos publicly to YouTube, you need to become highly involved, because YouTube is officially a social media site for people over thirteen years of age. (Kids under thirteen are supposed to go to YouTube Kids, but not many do.) Whenever your kids post content for others to view, like, and comment on, you've entered a whole different category of screen time, and the research about that is becoming crystal clear: monitor it and limit it heavily.

That brings us to the world of adolescents.

## Screen Limits for Adolescents: Ages Twelve to Nineteen

The reason I start with age twelve here instead of thirteen is because twelve is when many kids begin middle school, and that's a huge year of transition.

The screen limits for adolescents are similar to the screen limits for six- to eleven-year-olds in that there is no consensus among the experts on a certain number of hours. This becomes more difficult with adolescents because they're more likely to carry a screen with them almost every hour of the day.

How on earth do you track that?

Here's where I'll remind you once again: *rules won't raise your kids*. You don't *have* to track your kids' screen time. Neither the Bible nor the most current medical journals dictate that you spy on your kids and control their every move. In fact, both the Bible and most medical journals recommend another method: talk with your kids about this stuff . . . *a lot*!

Don't get me wrong. I'm not recommending no screen limits. I'm actually trying to let you off the hook a little bit. You don't need to monitor your kids 24/7. It's far better to do what we've been talking about throughout this book: first engage your kids in conversations about becoming screenwise, then set some fair and reasonable guardrails that will help them stay on course.

So what are some reasonable and loving screen limits for adolescents? Considering what most experts agree on, here are my recommendations:

- Don't allow devices in the bedroom at night. Period.

- Turn off screens one hour before bedtime.

- Don't allow social media until age thirteen. It's the law. (As you've already read in previous chapters.)

- Don't give kids their first smartphone until they reach high school *and* have read and discussed a book written to teenagers about becoming screenwise.

- Limit social media to just one or two hours per day, especially for girls.

- Set the default for social media profiles to *private*. Yes, even if your kid wants to become an influencer. But you might consider letting sixteen- or seventeen-year-olds have freedom in this area so they learn how to recognize predatory behaviors and navigate this dangerous landscape before they launch out on their own.

- If you notice other screen activities hurting your kids' relationships, grades, or exercise, set some reasonable limits to help maintain a healthy balance.

- Turn off screens and put them away during meals. Yes, Mom and Dad too.

- Create no-tech zones, such as bedrooms, the dinner table, and maybe even areas for reading.

Yes, you don't see a lot of specific screen-time limits in this list, other than "No screens one hour before bedtime" and "Limit social media to just one or two hours per day." That's because many of these loving limits depend on the kids, their exact ages, and their maturity level.

But don't underestimate the specificity of these recommendations, because as vague as some of them might seem, the simple "No devices in the bedroom at night" rule will probably keep most kids from spending hours upon hours on their screens daily.

Picture Natalie, the fourteen-year-old at the beginning of the chapter who averaged four to six hours of screen time per day, even though her parents told her, "Only two hours."

How would the screen limits I just listed help Natalie's parents?

1. If Natalie's parents had waited until high school to give their daughter a device, she would have been more mature and less vulnerable to many of the distractions and dangers phones present. Plus, she wouldn't have had to lie about her age to get on social media or immediately learn that the rules are "dumb" and easy to circumvent.

2. Natalie would be more equipped to make discerning decisions if her parents would dialogue with her about being screenwise. Natalie's parents have never done this. They just "threw her the keys." Where is Natalie supposed to learn these principles? On Netflix? How will kids learn this kind of discernment if parents never talk about it?

3. Natalie would clock far less screen time if her parents would collect her phone every night about an hour before bed. But Natalie has been given free rein, often staying on her phone late into the night, which makes her more tired, irritable, and even impulsive during the day. This spirals into even worse decision making on her device.

> *How will kids learn this kind of discernment if parents never talk about it?*

4. If Natalie's mom actually set screen-time limits on Natalie's social

media use (which can be done through parental controls), that would provide a little more accountability for Natalie with all the Instagram, YouTube, and TikTok time she is clocking. It would also make her more aware of how much time she's actually been spending on social media. Sure, Natalie might be able to sneak in time on social media using other devices and other usernames (as many kids do), but hopefully all of her conversations with Mom and Dad about the effects of social media would have an impact so she'd learn to make discerning screen-time decisions on her own. Isn't that what every parent wants?

5. If Natalie's parents created no-tech zones around the house, kept dinner sacred, and became proactive about hanging out together as a family, this would help Natalie value face-to-face relationships even more in her life and realize that people inside the room are far more important than the people outside.

6. Most importantly, all of these loving limits would minimize the number of hours Natalie is subjected to the pressurized environment of social media each day that sends her false messages like "You're not pretty enough," "You don't have enough followers," "Maybe if you acted a little more sexy, you'd get more likes."

If Natalie is like most young girls today, the hours she's devoting to her favorite screen activities are taking a toll on her mental health.

And here's the scary element of all this: Natalie is actually above the curve compared to most girls her age. She spends less time on screens and actually participates in a sport that gives her more than an hour of physical activity each day.

Don't underestimate the positive impact activity can have on your kids.

A group of researchers conducted a study with more than 4,200 adolescents ranging from twelve to sixteen years of age to see how their daily activities affected how they felt about themselves. The results were fascinating.[8]

Twelve-, fourteen-, and sixteen-year-olds wore accelerometers so researchers could track their movements. "The study found that every extra hour of daily activity helped to lower depressive symptoms by 7.8 to 11.1 percent, depending on the age of the child." In fact, depressive symptoms increased by nearly the same percentages "for every extra hour of sedentary behavior" the kids recorded. Sitting around staring at screens didn't help. "Adolescents with the highest amounts of inactivity during their teen years had depression scores over 28 percent higher than other children."[9]

Screen time matters.

So what might loving limits look like in your home?

## Applying Loving Screen Limits in Your Home

How can you apply these screen recommendations with your kids?

First, engage them in conversations about what healthy limits might look like. Don't just lay down the law. Discuss the why behind the limits. Maybe even practice what you've learned throughout this book about creating a climate of comfortable conversation about these issues:

1. When you read something in this book that piques your interest, bring it up at a family gathering. Break the ice with a fun question. For example, "If you could have a do-over for any moment of your life, what would you redo?"

2. Bring up the issue you'd like to talk about by reading a noteworthy paragraph or study. Then ask your kids' opinions. Listen; don't lecture. Just ask questions, such as . . .

   • Why do you think most experts recommend limiting the time on social media for teens?

- What screen limits do you think would be helpful for most teens?

3. Practice empathy by stepping into your kids' shoes and trying to understand their viewpoints and feelings. Don't criticize their responses; just listen.

4. Ask your kids, "What do you think is best? How would you solve the problem at hand?" Or, in this case, ask, "What screen limits would be most helpful for you?"

5. Delay correction or decisions. Actually walk away. Don't rush to set boundaries or impose a decision right away. Tell your kids you need some time to think and pray about the situation.

When you finish the book, add this step:

6. Set a time to talk about what you've read and make some decisions. Give your kids advance notice. You might say, "This Thursday we're going out for pizza to talk about how we can become screenwise."

As you engage in these discussions with your kids, pay attention to their ages, *because age and maturity matter.*

## No Rules Senior Year

If you look at the recommended screen limits in this chapter, you'll notice a principle that applies to all of parenting: start strict, then give more freedom as your kids mature.

When I was conducting research for my book *If I Had a Parenting Do-Over*, I asked hundreds of parents one simple question: "If you could go back in time and change one parenting practice, what would you do over?"

I was shocked at how many parents answered the same as I did: "I wish I hadn't been so strict with my teenager." The answer came in many forms:

- "I wish I hadn't made so many decisions for my teens, because it was like they never learned how to make decisions for themselves."

- "I held on too long. I tried to save my teens from hurt and ended up hurting them in the long run."

If you look at the guidelines in this chapter, they are superstrict with young kids: no screen time at all for kids under two years of age. Then the screen-time limits lighten up after age two: one or two hours a day. For preadolescents, screen time varies, but other limits help parents filter the quality and quantity of screen time. And finally, when kids enter adolescence, you begin to see a lot more about helping them learn how to make these screen-time decisions on their own.

I remember when my oldest daughter was in middle school and she was whining to me about one of my rules one day.

"Dad, all my friends can listen to this music!"

That's when I told her, "You might think I'm strict now, but all your friends are going to be jealous of you your senior year, because you're going to have no rules at all."

My daughter was silent for about ten seconds. Then she turned and said, "Oh, okay." She didn't even ask another question.

And I kept my word. I was very strict with my kids during middle school, but when they entered high school, they had more freedom, until both of my girls finally experienced no rules their senior year.

Yes, *no rules.*

Here's the thing. So many of us lay down rules until our kids leave the house. Then—*poof!*—like magic, they're completely free to do whatever they want. Chances are your kids won't call you from their college dorms and ask if they can watch the new HBO show their roommate is streaming. They're going to make that decision on their own, and the only question you can ask yourself right now is *Am I equipping them for that day?*

I let my girls experience no rules a year before they left for college. That included total freedom with their screens. They chose what they downloaded. They decided how much screen time was enough. I knew they'd be making these decisions on their own in college, so why not practice during their senior year of high school?

*No rules* didn't mean they could disrespect our family and smoke weed in the living room. In fact, not much changed.

I remember my daughter Ashley asking me, "Dad, can I spend the night at Rosie's house?"

I laughed and said, "I don't know. What do you think you should do?"

She inevitably replied, "Oh, that's right. No rules."

But then she started to do something very interesting. She'd ask me for advice. "Dad, what would you do if your friends put on a bad movie, and you don't want to get up, leave, and make a scene?"

That's where I eventually learned to resist my desire to lecture, or even limit, and *listen* instead. I would just ask, "What do you think is a good way to handle that?"

My daughters' senior years became way more about coaching than setting limits.

Limits don't raise your kids. Limits won't teach them how to make good decisions. They'll just help your kids steer clear of some pesky distractions. It's up to you to engage your kids in conversations about what healthy limits might look like. And it's up to you to model those limits in your own life.

Let me repeat that last sentence so we don't miss it: *It's up to you to model those limits in your own life.*

> **Limits don't raise your kids. Limits won't teach them how to make good decisions.**

Do you have no-tech zones for yourself?

Do you spend too much time scrolling through social media or bingeing on Netflix?

Do you ever find yourself looking at your phone when you're hanging out with your family (even if they might be doing it too)?

Do you let your phone keep you up at night?

If you think your own screen time is under control, try something. But first you'll need to pray and ask God to give you a humble spirit, because you don't want this exercise to turn into a fight. In fact, promise God you'll listen and not argue. Once you have a teachable mindset, ask your spouse, "Honey, are there any screen habits you wish I'd change?" Try the same with your kids. You might be surprised what they say.

It's extremely valuable for your kids to see this humble, teachable spirit from you. You can teach what you *know*, but you can only reproduce who you *are*.

## Discussion Questions

1. Where do your kids rack up the most screen time?

2. Jonathan listed several screen recommendations that experts seem to agree on. Which of these are the most difficult for you to enforce and why?

3. Is the guideline "Make sure your kids are close by when they're watching screens" realistic? How would this help?

4. Which of these screen limits is one you know you should enforce in your home? Why?

5. Which of these screen limits is something you might need to model with your own device use?

6. What do you think of Jonathan's "no rules senior year" guideline?

7. How can you engage your kids this week in conversations about what healthy screen limits might look like?

## CHAPTER 7

# "I See You"

*Teaching your kids to recognize predatory behaviors
and spot Creepy Basement Guy*

EMMA MET JAYDEN ON INSTAGRAM. Well, "met" is a little misleading, because she never met him face-to-face. But to Generation Screen, meeting online is "meeting."

Jayden was one of Emma's followers; he had "liked" several of her pics and eventually commented when she posted a new picture of her dog, Jake.

> **Jayden:** I didn't know you had a corgi. I've got a 4-year-old Pembroke named Olaf.
>
> **Emma:** OMG. Adorable name. Send me a pic.

And they started DMing each other. Jayden was a freshman at the high school Emma would eventually attend. Emma was twelve.

DMing led to texting, and before long the two were texting each other every evening, sometimes late into the night. Jayden and Emma watched the same TV shows and listened to the same music. They were a perfect match. Emma was truly smitten.

And Jayden distinctively seemed to "get" Emma like no other guy ever had. He listened, encouraged her, and told her she was beautiful. Emma had never experienced this before with the guys at school. They were all into themselves and video games. He was almost too good to be true.

Point of fact, he *was* too good to be true.

But Emma didn't see it.

She didn't consider that she had posted multiple pics of her corgi on her profile, and it was obvious she was a corgi lover. She didn't think about the fact that every little girl her age had seen the movie *Frozen* with the beloved character Olaf. She certainly didn't know that her music app of choice was connected to her social media, set on "public," of course, so everyone had access to every song she played and every playlist she had ever created. And she never really thought about all the times she posted countless stories about her Netflix binges. ("Starting season 9 of Grey's! Please let McSteamy be all right!")

Anyone with any presence on any of these apps would "get" Emma in ten minutes' time.

But Jayden knew the game, taking note of Emma's favorite pastimes, never advancing too quickly, and always saying the right things. When Emma told Jayden her frustrations with her parents, he consistently sympathized with her, validated her feelings, and made her feel special.

> **Jayden:** That sounds frustrating. My parents were the same way, but now I live with my Uncle Mike. He's awesome. He trusts me and understands.

Emma got used to hearing Uncle Mike's name in Jayden's texts.

"Uncle Mike and I went to the lake today . . ."

"Uncle Mike and I went out for ice cream . . . "

**Em:** I wish I had someone like that.

**Jayden:** Well, maybe you'll meet him someday when we go out.

Emma actually looked forward to meeting Jayden face-to-face. She was just waiting for the right moment, because she knew her parents wouldn't let her.

One night, after a particularly bad fight with her parents, Emma texted Jayden.

**Em:** Let's meet tonight.

**Jayden:** Sure. How will you get out?

**Em:** My window. I've done it before. My parents are stupid.

**Jayden:** Ha. Mine, too. What time do you want to meet?

**Em:** Midnight.

**Jayden:** Cool. I'm actually studying late tonight with a couple friends for a group project, but I'll be done by midnight.

The two of them decided to meet at the far corner of the Walmart parking lot. Public, but private.

At 11:40 p.m., Emma snuck out her window.

At 11:58 p.m., Emma was already waiting in the parking lot when she received a text.

**Jayden:** I just finished my group project, and I'm headed there now. I don't want you to wait alone, so I'm sending Uncle Mike to pick you up. Here's his pic.

And that's when "Jayden" sent a picture of himself.

Jayden was actually forty-two-year-old William. A quick Google search told him "Jayden" was the most popular baby name the year Emma was born. William had been playing the part of Jayden perfectly. His pics were all of another high school kid he was following from across the country. But none of that mattered now. Because now Emma was expecting "Uncle Mike." And that's why Emma didn't even hesitate to get in the car when William pulled up in the Walmart parking lot.

I heard Emma's story from her mom after one of my parenting workshops. Not all predators are adults posing as kids; in fact, most of these incidents are kids taking advantage of other kids. But there are also far too many adult predators who don't even feel the need to hide their age, as well as a smaller percentage who pose as kids, as in Emma's situation. All of them are predators.

The scary thing is that I hear stories like this almost everywhere I speak, even more so in recent years. Probably because we're living in the predators' golden age. You read that correctly. It's never been a more opportune time for predators than right now. I'm not trying to scare you. I just want you to be aware of this reality. Over the past couple of years, three events have aligned to create a "perfect storm" for predators to swoop in:

> *It's never been a more opportune time for predators than right now.*

1. Teen self-esteem is at a historic low, thanks in huge part to social media. And this isn't a small little blip in the data. In chapter 5, you read about the 84 percent increase in adolescent girls experiencing a major depressive episode in 2018. You also read about the 56 percent increase in suicide among young people between 2007 and 2017. The numbers are still increasing at unprecedented rates. Kids feel worse about themselves, and

they're looking for affirmation in the wrong places. And creepy predators are ready to fill that void.

2. Social media profiles are the most "public" they've been in years. As little as two years ago, it was almost common knowledge to set your Instagram on "private." Now try to tell kids to set their social media profiles on private, and they'll look at you like you're crazy. "Whaaaaa? No way! I need more followers." Kids are making themselves vulnerable by posting personal information for anyone and everyone to see. And all because they're seeking more likes and followers. Predators love this!

3. Smartphone ownership is at an all-time high. When I'm on high school and even middle school campuses, it seems as if almost every kid has a phone (even though statistically about nine out of ten do[1]), and they're all on social media (statistically 97 percent[2]). This is a predator's playground.

Think of what this means for predators. They don't have to drive their proverbial paneled vans to a mall or a playground to find vulnerable young people, and the more daring predators don't even need to creep up and peek in a young girl's bedroom window. Why do this when kids are posting everything a predator would ever want to see on their public, easily accessible social media profiles? And predators can see all of this from the privacy of their own homes, trailers . . . or mom's basement.

Some apps have even developed a reputation for having a predator problem, such as TikTok, which uses algorithms that track the kinds of videos users like to watch. Algorithms like this actually help pedophiles find more victims by steering Creepy Basement Guy to content he enjoys, like little girls dancing.[3]

Bottom line: predators are exploiting these opportunities while parents, police, and tech companies are scrambling to catch up.

So who are these predators?

## Three Categories of Predators

Here are the three categories of predators I see young people encountering today, starting with the most common.

### 1. The Teen "Toolbag"

I don't know if I'd call these kids "predators," but it's worth noting that every school I visit—and I mean literally every single one—has students who have exploited other students through their phones.

The most common scenario is when a guy asks a girl for a "nude." She eventually sends it, usually on Snapchat or some platform where pics disappear shortly after they're posted. But the guy screenshots the pic, and a week later, a month later, a year later—doesn't really matter when—he forwards the pic to a bunch of his friends, if not the whole school.

This happens all the time. And by "all the time," I don't mean it happens to every kid. I mean it happens in every school. In fact, an analysis of thirty-nine different studies with a total of more than one hundred thousand participants, showed that about 15 percent of kids under eighteen years of age sent "sexually explicit images, videos, and/or messages" (referred to as "sexts"), and 27 percent received them. (These numbers increase as kids get older, especially in their late teens.) On top of that, 12 percent of participants said they forwarded sexts without consent.[4]

Let me simplify it for you. About a third of kids under eighteen have received sexts, and about a third of those kids forward them to someone else. If your kid attends a small country school of one hundred kids, statistically, twenty-seven of them have received a sexually explicit image, video, or text message, and ten have forwarded it to others.

Anyone who forwards nude photos of a schoolmate is cruel, but typically there is at least one of these "toolbags" on every campus who initiates this kind of behavior without any consideration for the individual this kid is exploiting. I don't typically label these cruel teens as *predators*, but I do have a couple of other choice names I'd be tempted to call them, because the fallout is always painful. In most situations, the girl whose picture was taken is so embarrassed, she switches schools; and in many situations, she'll attempt suicide, and she doesn't typically give thirteen reasons why.

I visited a middle school campus a month ago and asked the principal, a friend of mine, "How's it going this year? Any incidents with phones yet?"

He sighed. "Well, I just broke up a fight because of one."

"What happened?"

"Well, it all began last week, actually. Two kids were, let's just say, engaged in a sexual act in one of the restrooms during class, when another girl walked in on them."

True story. I couldn't possibly make this stuff up.

"Let me guess," I said. "The other girl took a picture."

"Actually, no," he explained. "She hung an immediate U-turn, and by the time she got her phone out of her backpack, she was down the hall. But she immediately described what she saw on her social media, and within an hour the entire school knew."

"Did the two kids in the bathroom come to school the next day?" I asked.

"The girl didn't. I don't think she's coming back. Way too humiliated. But the boy did, and the reason I just broke up a fight is because all the guys keep teasing this guy for hooking up with this girl. Let's just say she wasn't on most guys' list of hotties at the school. So he tried to solve the problem with his fists."

I spoke in another city where three girls solicited a guy, asking him to send them a nude video of himself. They promised to reciprocate. This guy immediately filmed himself completely nude, and they forwarded the video to the entire school. They never had any intention of returning the favor.

This was a Christian school in the Bible Belt.

The whole school had to shut down because teachers couldn't even keep order in the classroom. Everyone was laughing, and the joking was out of control.

This isn't always kids who know each other; in fact, now that almost all teens are setting their social media profiles on public, the number of "stranger" teens asking other teens for nudes has increased greatly. It's not uncommon for girls to be solicited by other teens asking them to send nude photos. It's so common that our culture is constantly claiming it's "no big deal." For example, teen actress Zendaya played a teenager in a sexually charged HBO show titled *Euphoria*. In the pilot, her character, Rue, defended sending nudes, arguing, "I'm sorry. I know your generation relied on flowers and father's permission, but it's 2019, and unless you're Amish, nudes are the currency of love. So stop shaming us."[5]

If your kid doesn't feel this way, the pressure is on.

This is yet another reason to press the Pause button on giving your eleven- or twelve-year-old kid that phone. Not many people would label me extreme for saying that eleven-year-olds aren't really equipped to navigate this kind of harassment from friends and strangers.

But sadly, teens aren't the only ones exploiting teens.

## 2. Creepy Basement Guy

This is the guy your mother warned you about when you were a kid, but now he has a brand-new device with a high-speed connection.

Some of these guys are adults posing as teens, like the one who solicited Emma at the beginning of the chapter. But the majority of online predators actually don't hide the fact they're adults.[6] They just do what they can to groom, trap, or even "sextort" young people into giving them what they want.

The law enforcement friends I've made who work in ICAC (Internet Crimes Against Children) always tell me that when they catch these predators, they typically have conversations going on with dozens of kids at once, seeing which ones pan out and bailing out at the first sign of danger.

A youth worker I know was playing video games with his son. They were connected to his eleven-year-old nephew across the country and a couple of strangers. During game play, one of these strangers kept making inappropriate comments. My friend let a couple of the comments slide because some people tend to use foul language while gaming. But this guy began making some sexual comments. So my friend said, "Hey, man, how old are you?"

Immediately the guy disappeared from the game.

Many of these guys (and I say *guys*, because the vast majority of predators are males) are either really bold, dropping sexual hints and fishing for a response, or they're expert groomers. All of them have learned that young people want to feel noticed, heard, validated, and even attractive. And when an older adult gives them this attention, kids feel special and eventually safe enough to share more about themselves.

But so many of these guys work straight out of the pedophile's handbook. That's why it's important to teach our kids how to recognize predatory behaviors. In fact, in my *Teen's Guide to Face-to-Face Connections in a Screen-to-Screen World*, I warn young people to look out for specific grooming behaviors. Here are just a few of them:

- Predators almost always sympathize with the way you are feeling about something and affirm your feelings or choices. *Oh, I hate that. My parents used to say that to me too. You should totally sneak out.*

- Predators often try to drive a wedge in between [your] relationships with family or friends. *I would never treat you like that.*

- Predators often give excessive compliments or even send gifts or money.

- Predators try to find out your personal information. *I play volley-ball too. What school do you play for?*

- Predators will increasingly introduce sex into the conversation or show you pornography.

- Predators most often will eventually ask for "nudes" or secrets that they will then turn around and use to control you.[7]

I warn young people that if they ever see any of these grooming behaviors from someone online, they should tell their mom, dad, teacher, or youth pastor immediately. Even if they aren't sure.

Some of these tips seem obvious, but young people tend to think they're invincible. I just spoke on this topic at a banquet for a large youth organization, where I was equipping parents to help their kids recognize some of these predatory behaviors. The head of the organization told me afterward, "I'm amazed how many times we can warn kids about this stuff, and yet they completely ignore it. Last month we took a hundred kids on a trip and stayed in hotels each night. My adult chaperones had to sleep by the door because kids kept trying to sneak out to meet someone they had just met online that day."

But sometimes these predators are more than just some creepy guy wanting to hook up with a kid.

### 3. The Sex Trafficker

Sex traffickers might seem like the individuals I just described, since they use many of the same tactics. But these predators have streamlined these tactics into a business model.

I don't want to mislead you, so I'll be candid. Most sex traffickers target especially vulnerable kids who are escaping what they perceive to be a negative environment. The friends I have who work with organizations that fight sex trafficking all tell me the same thing: Sex traffickers typically target runaways, foster kids, or kids with addictions. Kids who are questioning their sexual identity are also more at risk because they often feel safer going to online sources and are afraid to tell anyone at home. Traffickers might start grooming kids the same way Creepy Basement Guy does, but their goal is to "sextort" them or get them to meet somewhere.

*Sextortion* is blackmailing a kid to do something sexual.

For example, I met a nurse whose niece was a foster kid. This young girl met a guy online who claimed he was a teenager. The two grew close, and it wasn't long before he asked for a nude photo. Once she sent a nude, everything changed. He threatened to send the photo to every one of her contacts, including her foster parents, unless she met with him. So she agreed.

"Just please don't send that pic to anyone," she pleaded.

When she went to meet him, he wasn't even the one who picked her up. She was trafficked to Vegas, where she was forced to prostitute herself for the weekend. The traffickers then used the video footage from those encounters to threaten her even more.

She was trafficked several times before she finally told her foster parents. The police removed her from that home, and the nurse I met adopted her.

Sextortion is a "particularly damaging form of online abuse."[8] In 2016, a Department of Justice report revealed that most perpetrators "target girls between the ages of 10 and 17, . . . conducting conversations online to build trust, asking for sexual photos, then using those photos as [a] basis for blackmail."[9] The report analyzed forty-three separate cases of sextortion. Two of the forty-three victims eventually committed suicide, and ten others attempted it.[10] Let those numbers sink in. That's more than one-fourth of the victims.

The initial contact between a teen and a sex trafficker almost always begins through a comment or DM on social media. Any friend or follower can typically DM your kid unsolicited unless you specifically go into the app and turn off direct messaging.

I spoke at a church where one of their high school girls was trafficked and eventually rescued. She responded to a "modeling opportunity" she received via Instagram. Her parents allowed her to go, but there was no agency at the address. She was abducted going into the building.

Months later, someone happened to see her downtown, drugged out of her mind. Her youth worker, who was an adventure-sports nut, went downtown, posed as a client, and rescued her. (They should turn that into a movie!)

I share these true stories every time I speak at school assemblies, and after my presentations, kids will often tell me their own experiences of strangers sending nude photos or requesting to meet. The crazy part of this is that whenever I speak at one of these schools, regardless of the size of the town, I'll look at the school's Instagram page, tap on "Followers," and begin looking through students' profiles. Whenever I find a picture of a student posing in a bikini or short shorts (they aren't difficult to find), I'll show it to school adminstrators, and we'll immediately scroll down to the comments. It's almost more common than not to find these types of messages:

> Looking good. DM me if you'd like to pursue modeling.

> Hot!!! DM if you'd like to become an influencer for us.

> Gorgeous. I've got connections if you'd like to earn some extra money. DM me.

I typically link the profile and send it to my ICAC contact in California, asking if any of the messages are legit.

She told me, "Modeling agencies aren't perusing high school kids' profiles looking for new clients. These are typically very suspicious. Assure these kids to definitely *not* meet up with any of these people."

## Protecting Your Kids from Predators

So how can you protect your kids from any of these predators? Here are a few tips:

- First and foremost, connect with your kids regularly so they feel loved, noticed, and heard. This might sound like a no-brainer, but think about it for a moment: most of the kids who respond to predators do so because they crave attention they aren't getting at home. Predators are masters at listening and validating your kids' feelings. Are you?

> *Predators are masters at listening and validating your kids' feelings. Are you?*

- Don't freak out. I know, you just read a chapter about pedophiles and sexual predators trying to abduct your children. But if you freak out, your kids will think, *Mom doesn't understand.* Or maybe, *Dad isn't safe. He's losing it again.* Overreacting doesn't protect your kids; it actually puts them in more danger.

- Turn the temptation to overreact into *interaction.* Talk with your kids about this issue calmly. Don't try to scare them. They don't need to be afraid; they need to be aware. Take your kids through a teen's guide to becoming screenwise and share true stories about these kinds of situations, including practical tips that will help your kids recognize predatory behaviors.

- Talk with your kids about their social media profiles. Friend or follow them on social media. Be present in their online lives. Many social media platforms give you the option of setting notifications on your phone whenever one of your "friends" posts something. Don't post about your kids or comment; this will just embarrass them. Don't even "like" every post. Instead, talk with your kids about their posts and focus on encouraging them more than correcting them.

- Help your kids modify the privacy settings on all of their social media platforms, including the chat or communication settings for their games. Many platforms default to "public." Teach your kids how to switch those settings to "private" and explain why it's important not to give strangers free access to all of their pictures.

- Help young kids set the controls on their gaming devices and apps so they don't connect with strangers. (Yes, kids' games like *Roblox* and *Minecraft* have chat features.) Help older kids limit their chatting with strangers and become aware of predatory behaviors.

- Teach your kids to avoid posting locations of the places they frequent and to never post pictures in front of your house.

- Also teach them to be careful whom they share personal information with. They should never share their phone number or address, or even their last name, with someone they meet online.

- And yes, I'm going to say it again: don't allow their phones or any devices in the bedroom. Predators love late-night conversations.

- Don't be afraid to do occasional spot checks. Not every day, and probably not even every week. But every once in a while, if you notice one of your kids engrossed in a texting conversation, say, "Show me." This works best if you tell your kids you'll be doing this when they first ask for their own phones. As you educate them about the dangers, you can tell them honestly, "I know you might not like it, but if you want a phone, Dad and I will have access to that phone whenever we want. And the more you earn our trust, the less we'll look at your phone. In fact, our plan is to not ever look at your phone your senior year."

- If you discover that your kids have connected with a predator or engaged in inappropriate conversations, again, don't freak out. Don't make them feel like it's their fault. Become a safe source they can come to if they mess up. No, this doesn't mean you won't correct them; it just means you won't shame them. (We'll talk more about how to do this in chapter 9.)

## Creating a Climate of Comfortable Conversation

Don't forget to practice what you've learned throughout this book about creating a climate of comfortable conversation in your home:

1. When you read something in this book that piques your interest, bring it up at a family gathering. Break the ice with a fun question. For example, "What's the funniest video you've ever seen online?" And then ask, "What's the weirdest thing you've ever seen online?"

2. Bring up the issue you'd like to talk about by reading a note-worthy paragraph or study. Then ask your kids' opinions. Listen; don't lecture. Just ask questions, such as . . .

   - Which of the three types of predators do you think is most common? Why?

- Why do you think young people are more vulnerable to these kinds of predators today?

- Why do you think twelve out of forty-three teenagers committed or attempted to commit suicide after being victims of sextortion?

- How can someone avoid these dangers?

3. Practice empathy by stepping into your kids' shoes and trying to understand their viewpoints and feelings. Don't criticize their responses; just listen.

4. Ask your kids, "What do you think is best? How would you solve the problem at hand?"

5. Delay correction or decisions. Actually walk away. Don't rush to set boundaries or impose a decision right away. Tell your kids you need some time to think and pray about the situation.

When you finish the book, add this step:

6. Set a time to talk about what you've read and make some decisions. Give your kids advance notice. You might say, "This Thursday we're going out for pizza to talk about how we can become screenwise in this house."

Next, we'll look at how open communication partnered with a few parental controls can help you and your kids on this journey.

## Discussion Questions

1. Jonathan suggested that three events have aligned to create a "perfect storm" for predators to swoop in: teen self-esteem is at a historic low, social media profiles are the most "public" they've been in years, and smartphone ownership is at an all-time high. Which of these events have you noticed most?

2. Why do you think 15 percent of young people send "nudes" or sexual texts (sexts)? What's the draw to do this? How can we open the door for dialogue about this with our kids?

3. Have you ever talked with your kids about online predatory behaviors? Which ones do you think your kids most need to be aware of?

4. Why do you think Jonathan's first tip for protecting your kids from predators is "Connect with your kids regularly so they feel loved, noticed, and heard"?

5. How does your freaking out actually make your kids more vulnerable to predators?

6. How can you create a climate of comfortable conversation about predators with your kids this week?

CHAPTER 8

# Where Parental Controls Matter

*The settings that help keep your kids safe*
*and block distractions*

I HAVE TWO FRIENDS I'll call Don and Brian. They parented in completely opposite ways, especially regarding the number of parental controls they applied to their children's devices.

Don pretty much let his kids do anything. Don Jr. could watch any movies or shows he wanted—literally *any*. He could listen to any music—and he did. He could download any apps. You name it, Don's kids had it.

His kids were the ones other kids would bring up in arguments with their parents: "But Don Jr. can do it!"

If your kids saw an inappropriate movie, and you asked, "Where did you see *that*?" it would eventually come out, "I saw it over at Don Jr.'s."

Don's kids got phones before anyone else, and they immediately signed up on all the popular social media platforms. Don didn't use any parental controls at all.

"They've gotta learn for themselves," he'd say.

And they did. Often the hard way.

Brian was the antithesis of Don. Brian monitored everything his kids did. They were only allowed to watch PG movies, using a Christian movie-filtering service that blocked out every curse word and any sensual scenes. They were only allowed to listen to Christian music. Blatantly Christian music. If the song went mainstream, it wasn't Christian.

Brian's kids didn't even get phones until they were sixteen, and when they did, Brian installed monitoring software on all their devices that showed him everything he could possibly want to know about his kids' online activities at any moment.

He demonstrated it for me once.

"Look," he said, pulling up the software on his phone. "Right now Brian Jr. is over at Don Jr.'s house. He's been there two hours. The last app he used was Minecraft, for thirty minutes." Brian looked up from his phone proudly. "Brian Jr.'s phone limits him to just thirty minutes of Minecraft every day."

(What Brian didn't know was that Brian Jr. and Don Jr. were both watching HBO at that very moment on Don's TV.)

Brian tried to monitor *everything*! If someone invented a drone that would fly over your kids' heads and watch their every move, Brian would have it.

It's funny when I think about it. Almost every other parent I've met falls somewhere between Don and Brian. I've met very few parents as carefree and hands-off as Don. And I've met drill sergeants who didn't hold a candle to Brian. In fact, if you've ever heard someone say, "Big Brother is watching," I'm pretty sure they were talking about Brian. Brian *is* Big Brother.

Don—no parental controls at all.

Brian—every parental control imaginable, including monitoring software.

So what about you? Where are you on the parental-control scale compared to Don and Brian?

How many parental controls are too many?

## The Right Number of Parental Controls for Your Kids

By this point in the book, many of you are starting to form educated opinions about what might actually help your kids learn to become screenwise. I say "educated" because I've taken you on a journey in the last seven chapters in which we've analyzed some of the most current research about your kids' physical and mental health. You've seen the wisdom of teaching your kids to become screenwise *before* giving them their first screens. You've also seen the wisdom of delaying the age they first get social media, limiting the hours they spend on certain apps, and helping them avoid some of the distractions today's screens create (a little too gratuitously, sadly).

Parental controls offer some accountability in these areas—as long as they are *not* a substitute for communication and connection.

Let me say it another way: parental controls can actually be quite helpful, when partnered with open communication. They actually become weaker and less effective when parents overly rely on them to raise their kids.

No, I'm not trying to talk you out of using parental controls. I just want to be clear that controls are only as good as the conversations that precede them.

So how much control should parents apply?

I don't know what it is, but for some reason moms and dads get a little weird about parental controls. Choosing these limits can almost become a political minefield. Everyone disagrees about exactly how much control to apply, and they don't really understand the people who think differently than they do. (Imagine having to write a chapter about which parental controls are helpful. I'm doomed right out of the gate.)

People become advocates of the controls they use. "How come those parents don't use the software we use? They really should try Digital Leavenworth. Digital Leavenworth provides by far the best parental controls!" (That's not real software, by the way. I made it up.)

In all of my research and years helping parents, I've noticed two realities about parental controls, especially in recent years.

## Two Uncomfortable Realities about Parental Controls

### 1. In Most Situations, the More Monitoring Software Parents Use, the Less They Engage in Dialogue with Their Kids.

Parental controls and monitoring software are two different degrees of control. Parental controls restrict access to specific content or limit screen time. Most of these controls are included in modern-day devices. Monitoring software is something extra that enables parents to actually peek in on what their kids are doing on all of their devices in real time.

I haven't noticed many negative effects when parents use a reasonable number of parental controls, especially if they lighten those controls as their kids grow older and become more mature. But I *have* observed negative results when parents put too much focus on monitoring software. No, not in every case, but typically, the more a parent relies on "spyware" to monitor their kids, the less their kids feel trusted and the less likely they are to open up with their parents. Yes, I've seen exceptions to this. But honestly, many well-intentioned parents who monitor their kids hurt the relationships.

Bottom line: It's the age-old balance between bonding and boundaries. Kids need boundaries, but not at the expense of bonding. Kids need rules, but not in place of relationship. Kids don't need prison guards; they need parents.

That being said, I'm definitely a big advocate for parental controls, especially the first few years after kids get screens. But I'm *not* a big fan of monitoring their every move.

Plus, even if you monitor your kids as much as Brian does, you have to realize that there are limitations.

## 2. Parental Controls Are Far from Foolproof

Mere parental controls don't work.

Read that sentence again. *Mere* parental controls. Remember what I said at the beginning of this chapter: parental controls can actually be quite helpful, *when partnered with open communication.*

Bottom line: You need both. Both work well together.

Sadly, some parents hope that parental controls and monitoring software will do the job for them. So they miss out on opportunities to dialogue with their kids about truth. This is a huge tragedy. Your conversations about God's design for sex and intimacy will be far more effective than any porn filters. Plus, kids frequently find ways around parental controls and content filters. I've seen far too many examples: using hidden devices and duplicate social media accounts, changing the time zone on the phone to extend screen time, or factory resetting their devices to bypass controls and then coming up with a sad story to explain it.

One mom told me her son hid inappropriate content in "the cloud" and would access it after hours. The more difficult part of all this is the fact that with a simple Google search, your kids can access all kinds of tutorials on how to do many of these hacks.

Point of fact: parental controls don't block everything.

I couldn't possibly tell you how many times I've heard a parent tell me, "I've got this handled. I know everything my kids are doing. They aren't seeing anything without me knowing about it." Honestly, I hear that from at least one parent in almost every city.

Please don't become overconfident about the use of parental controls and spyware. Those who have been reading this book from the beginning have read these words again and again: *Rules won't raise your kids.* And porn filters won't either. In fact, any expert on the subject will tell you that you can set all the porn filters and screen limits you want, and yet not only will your kids *still* encounter objectionable material, but they will also have to make a decision in the moment: *Should I keep watching this?*

Have you equipped your kids to make that decision? Or have you just tried to filter or block every possible distraction headed their way?

Let me say it another way . . . and you may not like it.

If your kids want to see porn, *they will see porn.* You can even install a special router that blocks porn at the Wi-Fi level, set every control available on their phone, and buy devices and software that will limit every kilobyte of content on every device in the house, and your son's friend can *still* send him a nude pic via text or airdrop. Or he could just walk up to your son, hold out his own unblocked phone, and say, "Hey, check this out!"

This is far more common than you think. I recently met parents who set every possible blocker on their son's device with such confidence that they let him take it into the bedroom every night. Months later they discovered that he had found a way around the blocker and had been looking at porn each night.

I'll say it again: *Mere* parental controls don't work.

So what does?

## The Good News

You can help prepare your kids for these moments, starting with your conversations about becoming screenwise and some reasonable parental controls that will hold your kids accountable.

I'll say it again: parental controls can actually be quite helpful, *when partnered with open communication*. This communication typically happens through continual conversations at dinner, long car rides, or while stirring a campfire under the stars.

Ask Phil and Katy, who have three girls—one in high school, one in middle school, and one in elementary school. Their family loves screens, but Phil and Katy wisely waited to give their girls handheld devices. In fact, only the oldest girl, Grace, has a smartphone right now; the other two know they'll get one the summer before high school.

Grace didn't just wake up and get a smartphone when she turned fourteen. She and her mom went out for breakfast every Thursday morning during the summer and worked through a teen's guide to social media, discussing a chapter each week.

Phil and Katy didn't just lay down a bunch of rules; they got to the why behind many of the rules. So when Grace first got her phone, she was open to many of the parental controls her parents set up from the beginning, such as having to ask her mom to enter a password before downloading any app, or time limits on certain apps like Instagram.

But Grace was still a teenager, so she actually disagreed on a few of the limits. For example, she didn't like that she couldn't have TikTok.

"The answer isn't no," her mom said. "It's not yet. As you get older, you'll be able to make some of these decisions for yourself."

Grace wasn't thrilled with that answer. But she did appreciate that she was gaining more freedom each year.

Every night, Grace would bring her phone and her laptop into her parents' bedroom and connect them both to the charger in the master closet. Then she'd fetch them first thing each morning.

Phil and Katy never bought any extra monitoring software for Grace's devices. Grace was pretty mature by the time she got the phone, and she was demonstrating wisdom and trustworthiness in her decision making. Frankly, the controls that came with her phone were pretty detailed. Phil and Katy didn't even use half of them. But the ones they did use seemed to do a pretty good job keeping Grace from becoming too entrenched in her phone.

That's what a lot of parents are discovering today. Many devices offer pretty sufficient parental controls if you're already doing everything else we've talked about in this book so far. Here's a recap:

- Make sure young kids are close by when they're watching screens, not off in a bedroom by themselves.

- Ask your kids regularly about what they're watching and what games or apps they're playing with. Dialogue about what they're seeing.

- Watch programming with your children and talk about what you see.

- Wait to give your kids phones until they enter high school.

- Read through a book together, such as *The Teen's Guide to Social Media and Mobile Devices*, and teach your kids how to become screenwise *before* you give them a phone.

- Create no-tech zones, such as bedrooms and the dinner table.

- Turn off screens one hour before bedtime.

- Don't allow devices in the bedroom at night. Period.

Take a close look at each of these screen guidelines. Notice that not one of them requires you to use any of the parental controls on your kids' devices. They just require you to be involved in your kids' lives.

Does this mean you don't need to use parental controls on your kids' devices?

Unfortunately, no. Because the recommendations you've read throughout this book also include wise principles like these:

- Don't allow social media until age thirteen. It's the law.

- Limit social media to only one or two hours per day, especially for girls.

- Turn off the chat or live-play feature for video games. Young kids shouldn't be chatting with strangers on their gaming systems.

Here's where parental controls can be a big help: applying communication settings, blocking the downloads of certain apps, and limiting the hours of screen time.

Each device your kids own has parental controls. Your son's gaming system has the ability to block chatting with strangers while online in multiplayer mode. Just google "How do I block chatting on Xbox?" or whatever system you own, and you'll find these settings pretty easy to change. Your daughter's iPad has Screen Time settings as well that can block inappropriate content, limit hours of play, or do almost anything else.

Some parents have had success buying one parental control unit they can connect to their router that allows them to set limits on all devices from one app. These controls at the router level can be pretty effective when your kids are relying on the internet and/or Wi-Fi for devices that don't have their own internet or data plans. Once kids have their own phones (or have visiting friends with their own phones), these parental controls become a little less effective.

When kids have mobile devices, many parents find the inherent parental controls on those devices to be pretty efficient.

But like most loving limits, these controls vary by age.

## Age Matters

If you're a parent of a five-, a seven-, and a nine-year-old, and they don't have their own screens yet, you can breathe a sigh of relief right now. This process will be much easier for you. You have all the power. The moment they start begging for a device, you can begin prepping them by saying this:

> Well, owning a phone and getting social media is a huge responsibility, and responsibility is like trust. It's earned, not given. So if you want a phone, we'll have the passwords, and you'll begin with very limited access. The more you grow, mature, and demonstrate trust, the more access you'll get. And my goal is that you'll have no rules or limitations at all your senior year.

This is a much easier sell when your kids don't have devices yet. And setting parental controls on your eight-year-old's device is easier as well.

I can hear your question now: "What do you mean my eight-year-old's device? I thought I shouldn't buy my child a device until high school!"

In a perfect world, yes, you shouldn't. But in a postquarantine era where distance learning is a growing reality, many of our kids' schools have issued laptops or tablets. If this is the case, don't just hand these devices to your kids (don't just "throw them the keys").

The good news is that setting parental controls for an eight-year-old is much easier, because it's not so much about *choosing what you block*; it's more about *choosing just a few things you'll allow.*

If my eight-year-old *needed* a laptop for school, I would start by setting a strong password and then block literally everything on the computer so no one could download anything or browse anywhere—or basically do anything! Then I'd find out what my child needs for school and slowly unblock those few things. If you want your kids to be able to access a few innocent websites, download the web browser of your choice and set that browser so it can only go to the three websites you allow.

Eight-year-olds don't need to be navigating the web freely.

But what if you're the parent of teens *and* tweens who've already had free rein with their phones and have used social media for years? If that's the case and you want to make some changes now, the process will take time, energy, and patience. It's a little more difficult to take something away once your kids have already been using it.

Here's yet another instance where you'll want to practice what you've been learning throughout this book. You'll need to open up the door for dialoguing with your kids about loving limits that are healthy for them and their future.

- *Don't* take your kid's phone away and simply declare, "Whoops. My bad. I shouldn't have given you this in the first place."

- *Don't* install a bunch of passwords on your kid's phone one day and say, "Good luck getting on your social media platform now. Ha!"

- *Don't* delete a bunch of apps and say, "You shouldn't have downloaded this garbage anyway."

If your kids already have devices, hopefully you've been practicing the steps you've read again and again in this book. Have you created a climate of comfortable conversation so your kids can become screenwise? If you have, then you've already been talking with them about . . .

- what age young people should get a phone,
- what age young people should be on social media,
- why phones and bedrooms are not a good mix,

- what the effects of social media are, especially on girls, and
- what reasonable and helpful screen limits are.

As you've discussed these issues with your kids, hopefully you've not only shared research on the matter but have also asked your kids for their opinions and listened to them, making sure they feel heard and understood. And if you took my advice, you resisted laying down the law right then but waited, actually getting up and walking away, saying, "I need some time to think and pray about this."

Finally, I recommended setting a family meeting where you tell your kids what you've decided and implement some house rules to help them on their journey to becoming screenwise.

At this meeting, you'll not only share many of the loving limits we discussed earlier in the book (including "no screens in the bedroom after 8:00 p.m."), but you'll also add some helpful parental controls on your kids' devices.

The question is, which controls will help them?

## Give It a Try

One of the best pieces of advice I give parents is to google the parental controls for your kids' devices. You might type in "parental controls for the iPhone 36." (I wonder when that phone will come out?) You'll most likely find numerous articles and YouTube videos featuring some guy wearing a *Star Wars* T-shirt telling you everything you need to know.

And honestly, you can learn a lot by just clicking on the parental controls on your own devices and trying them out. You'll find all kinds of stuff you didn't even realize they had, from screen limits to content filters. It took me less than ten minutes to learn how to turn on my device's parental controls, require a password to download any app, limit

Instagram to just thirty minutes a day, and go into Downtime mode at eight o'clock every night.

## It's All about the Passwords

As you begin tapping around your kids' devices, the first and probably most important thing you'll realize is that most parental controls are powerless without a good password. I've heard countless stories from parents about their kids hacking their passwords.

Kids are smart! They only need to see you key in the sequence 1-2-3-4 once on the phone, and they now have access to everything.

That's one of the things about working in youth ministry as long as I have. You overhear kids talking to each other about this stuff, and it's kind of funny.

"My parents think I don't know their password, but it's their anniversary. Duh!"

"My parents' password is our phone number. Took me like three tries to figure that one out."

"Mine is my address."

And, yes, those are some of the most common passwords.

Here's my recommendation. Use something totally random. And random means something that isn't from your favorite movie, song, or TV show. If you're a *Star Wars* nerd, your password better not be THX1138. If you always have the eighties' station playing in your home, your password better not be 8675309.

By random I mean, do you remember a number there is no way your kids have ever heard, like your first phone number? What about your neighbor's license-plate number? (Take a picture of your friend's car and mix it in with a batch of photos on your phone. Your kid will most likely not notice.)

My point is this: take more than ten seconds to choose a password you're sure your kids could never guess.

Another thing you must consider is keeping that password private. Here are a few recommendations:

1. Don't write your password down anywhere. Your kids will find it. I've heard them talking about it.

2. Don't ever say it aloud to your spouse, even if you think your kids can't hear you. Again, it only takes once.

3. Don't give in when you're doing dishes and your hands are immersed in suds, and you think, *I'll just tell my daughter the password really quick so she can access something, and I'll remember to change it later.* Because most parents forget, and more importantly, your daughter now has a clue about the kinds of passwords you're using.

If you think these tips sound ridiculous, they just might be. But the fact is, there are plenty of you reading this right now whose password is 0-0-0-0, or your birthday, or your son's birthday, or the letters that spell out your daughter's name. (Did I get it yet?) And you might as well not have parental controls at all if your kids know the password.

So put a little effort into a strong password for your parental controls, and make sure your kids can't ever discover it. (Again, if you don't know how to set the password, google "setting parental controls on . . ." and enter each of your kids' devices. I guarantee you'll find several articles, blogs, and even YouTube videos telling you how to set those controls for your kids' specific devices. And one of the steps will inevitably be setting a password. This is where you choose a strong password your kids don't know.)

Don't confuse parental controls with the screen-lock password.

Chances are, your kids' devices, like yours, will require another password just to unlock the screen. Let your kids choose this password, because they need to punch it in about fifty times a day. But you and your spouse need to know it too.

Make that fact clear from the beginning. This phone isn't your kid's diary. It's not her private little world with a Kids Only sign hung on the door. This isn't that kids' channel on TV where Mom and Dad are idiots controlled by ingenious little brats. The phone is a privilege, just like driving a car. My guess is you're not going to let your twelve-year-old drive wherever he wants, and I'm 100 percent sure you're not going to let him tell you, "I'm not even telling you where I'm going!"

But the parental controls and screen-lock passwords aren't the only passwords you need to know.

## Individual App Passwords

So far you have one password your kids don't know: the parental-controls password. And if your kid's device uses a screen lock, that will be a password both you and your kid know. But individual apps sometimes require passwords as well.

So when you finally let your daughter get Instagram, she'll create a password. When she first opens her account, I think it's a good idea for you to know that password.

If you let her have Snapchat, make sure you know that password.

If you let her have TikTok, know that password too.

Again, opinions vary. Some parents think it's way too "Big Brother" to know every one of their kids' passwords. Personally, I'd rather start out strict. For example, I'd want to know everything if I were giving my fourteen-year-old daughter her first phone as a high school freshman. Then I'd lighten up as she proved herself trustworthy, a segue from a lot of control to very light control her junior year, and finally no rules her senior year.

But I start strict.

After you set all the passwords, a good place to begin with parental controls is setting the various screen limits typically found in the device settings. On most phones and tablets, these settings give parents the opportunity to limit screen time, filter content, and even control downloads.

Let's look at some of the basic parental-control settings you'll want to consider using.

## Recommended Parental Controls

In this section, I obviously won't be able to give you the particulars of every keystroke and swipe specific to your kids' devices or the software you purchased, because there are so many. But don't worry. I can still provide you with timeless broad strokes that you'll be able to use with any device.

Here are the controls I personally recommend:

### 1. Permission to Download and/or Delete Apps

When your kids first get a device, set a strong parental-control password, and then modify it so they can't download any app without a password. This requires your kids to come to you and ask permission to download that new social media app they want so badly—"Mom, can I have TikTok?"

Then you can apply what you learned in chapter 5 and answer, "I don't know. Let's check it out together."

I love it when parental controls create conversations.

You'll find this setting in a Parental Control or Screen Time setting on your kid's device, maybe labeled something like "Content & Privacy

Restrictions." Apple actually gives you the choice to require passwords to install apps, or you can set it so a password is required to download or delete any apps.

When your kids are young, don't allow either without a password. But as they get older and become more mature, consider allowing them to download apps without a password, but not delete them. Your kids will experience some freedom because they don't have to ask permission to download apps, but they do have to ask before they can delete that inappropriate app they downloaded. This helps you move from a position of control to a position of accountability.

But there's another privacy setting to consider.

## 2. Location Services Feature

The Location Services feature tells others where your kids are at any moment. Don't turn these off, because if you do, you'll never be able to use helpful features like "Find my iPhone" if your kids lose their devices, or other Find features your specific device might offer. But do go into each app and turn off specific Locations Services as needed.

For example, if your kids have Snapchat, they might have opted into a fun feature called Snap Map. This feature allows kids to share their locations with their friends on a real-time map. It's fun if they're sharing their locations with true friends they've met face-to-face and trust. But sadly, young people today tend to friend strangers. So now David Berkowitz can see exactly where your daughter is spending the night because it shows up in real time on a Snap Map.

If your kids want to use the Snap Map feature safely, they can go into the settings and turn it off completely or set it so only specific family and friends can see where they are at any moment.

These are good conversations to have with your kids. And you can help them set up Location Services limits for each of their apps.

### 3. Content Restrictions

Most devices have content restrictions that allow you to choose ratings for movies, music, TV shows, books, and apps. For example, you could set restrictions so your kids can't listen to songs marked "explicit." You could even make it so they're only allowed to download apps rated for ages nine and up instead of ages twelve and up. Then they won't be able to download most of the popular social media apps they want. (Or, as we just discussed, you can make it so they can't download any apps.)

Another feature you can restrict is web content. Many devices allow you to block adult websites. But with young kids, you can even set restrictions so they can only browse "allowed websites," and you can select which websites to allow.

Again, most devices offer a lot of content control. I'd encourage you to play around with this feature and test its effectiveness.

I also like to set limits within some of the entertainment apps. For example, if you allow your kids to have Netflix on their devices, make sure they do *not* have your Netflix password, and use settings so your kids can only see movies or TV shows with the ratings you choose.

The same applies with social media apps like TikTok. If you do allow your kids to have this app, make use of its Restricted Mode. No, this doesn't cut out all of the language and sensual material, but it does trim it a bit.

Most apps offer some sort of parental controls or even "digital well-being" settings. But these don't always help you limit *how long* kids spend on any of these apps.

### 4. App Limits

Many devices have parental-control settings that allow you to set time limits for specific apps or categories of apps. This is nice, because some apps don't offer adequate limits within their own settings. But you can use the device's parental controls to set a limit so your kids can only be on YouTube thirty minutes a day and on Instagram and Snapchat another thirty minutes combined. This is a great way to limit how much time your kids are spending on social media on a specific device.

In addition to limiting the amount of time kids spend on apps, you can also limit the hours kids spend on their devices.

### 5. Downtime Mode

In addition to limiting the amount of time kids spend on apps, you can also limit the hours kids spend on their devices.

Apple's Downtime feature allows you to set it so that a device, or specific apps you choose, will basically shut down for the night. You can select the exact downtime for each device or app. Other devices have similar settings.

I've heard some parents justify allowing their kids to have their phones in their bedrooms because of this setting. That's putting a lot of trust in parental controls. These are the parents who end up telling me stories about how their kids did a factory reset on their devices because they were so desperate to use them.

You can avoid all of that by simply collecting screens at night. Don't even expose your kids to the temptation, especially in a world where porn is just a tap or swipe away.

These are just some of the parental controls devices offer. As you explore your kids' devices, you might find more (or fewer) controls you want to apply. You make the call.

## The Best Porn Blocker

Parental controls are helpful, but let me remind you of the best porn blocker available: conversations with your kids about sex and intimacy.

I can't emphasize it enough. Parental controls are only as good as the conversations that precede them. Even though content filters can do a pretty good job keeping your kids from accessing inappropriate websites, your kids still need to know *why.*

And the answer isn't "Because I said so."

> **Parental controls are only as good as the conversations that precede them.**

Your kids might honestly wonder, *What's the harm in just looking at pictures of naked people?*

That's a good question—and it deserves a good answer. Scripture is where we should go for these answers, in all their explicit detail.

Take a peek at Proverbs 5:18-19 (NLT):

Let your wife be a fountain of blessing for you.
   Rejoice in the wife of your youth.
She is a loving deer, a graceful doe.
   Let her breasts satisfy you always.
   May you always be captivated by her love.

Let me assure you. This passage gets the attention of most young people. I use it a lot when a guy is struggling with sexual temptation. Like when guys ask me, "Why is porn sooooo tempting?"

I always answer this way:

Because God loves you so much that He gave you an amazing
gift to enjoy with one woman for life. The gift is sex. And it's so
amazing, in fact, that many people don't want to wait until they
meet that right person, or they think, *This is so good with one
person; I bet it's even better with more than one person.* But eventually
they find out that God actually knew what He was doing when
He designed you for a sexual relationship with just one person.

Often I'll turn to this Proverbs 5 passage and say, "Scripture is pretty clear about it right here." And then I'll read those verses.

I'll be honest. Those verses scare a lot of parents. They think, *I don't want to show my son a verse about breasts!*

Please reconsider. In a world of explicit lies, your son needs the explicit truth.

These verses are spoken to some men who are looking around at other women. The author of this proverb offered some amazing wisdom: instead of looking around at other women, remember your wife and how beautiful she is.

Here's where the Bible gets specific, and your son will actually appreciate it: "Enjoy your wife's breasts. Let them satisfy you."

*In a world of explicit lies, your son needs the explicit truth.*

That's some pretty steamy stuff.

But don't stop reading there. Here's what Proverbs 5:20 (NLT) says:

Why be captivated, my son, by an immoral woman,
or fondle the breasts of a promiscuous woman?

It doesn't get much clearer than that: Enjoy your wife's breasts; don't enjoy other women's breasts.

Here's where I would ask my son some basic questions:

What does the Bible tell us to enjoy?
What does the Bible warn us about?
Where are some places that guys might become distracted by other women's breasts today?

Very often, guys will cite porn as a place where they might encounter these distractions. This Proverbs 5 passage gives great perspective on why it eventually hurts us to look at another woman's breasts.

The purpose of this chapter on parental controls isn't about giving your kids the sex talk, although there it is (just think of it as bonus material). At this point in the conversation, I'd actually explain the difference between adultery (sex outside of marriage), sexual immorality (sexual activity when you aren't married yet), and lust (imagining sex). Hit Jesus' teaching on lust in Matthew 5:28 and maybe some good advice about fleeing sexual temptation in 2 Timothy 2:22. (My books *Sex Matters* and *The Guy's Guide to Four Battles Every Young Man Must Face* go into more detail about God's design for sex and intimacy.)

The point is, our kids need much more than porn blockers. They need to understand what porn is, why it's unhealthy, and what to do if they encounter it. Porn blockers can help your kids "flee" unwanted distractions, but ultimately your conversations about God's design for sex and intimacy are going to lay the foundation for their decision making when those temptations arise.

Are you having these conversations with your kids?

## Less Is More

My brother just called me as I was sitting here writing this, and he asked, "What are you doing?"

"Writing a chapter about parental controls," I answered.

"Oh, wow," he said, sounding a little more curious than I expected. "What are you recommending?" (His kids are twelve and fourteen.)

Without hesitation I answered, "Far fewer controls than I used with my kids." And then I went on to say, "If I had it to do over, I'd spend far less time trying to block out the world's lies and far more time sharing the Word's truth."

Think about it for a moment. If you end up spending more time checking the websites your kids visit than you do talking with them about what Jesus taught about how we treat others, something's out of balance.

I made that mistake.

And now everywhere I go, I try to warn people to put bonding before boundaries, love before limits, and connection before correction.

Earlier this year, a church brought me back to teach another parenting workshop. I was mingling with moms and dads before the workshop when a dad approached me.

"You don't know me," he said, "but I came to your workshop last year. I just wanted to thank you. You saved my relationship with my daughter Jessica."

Needless to say, he had my attention.

"Wow," I replied. "Thanks so much for the encouragement. What was it that I said?"

"Well, last year before coming to your workshop, my wife and I had pretty much decided that we weren't going to ever give our kids phones or let them have screens of any kind."

I gave him the Dr. Phil question: "So how was that working for ya?"

He laughed. "It wasn't."

"How old were your kids?" I asked.

"Eight, ten, and then Jessica. She's the oldest and was thirteen at the time."

"So what happened?"

"Jessica was the only one in her friend group who *didn't* have a phone. Literally the only one. She would beg us for one every day, sometimes in tears. We didn't budge."

"So what changed?"

"Last year when you told us about keeping our eyes on the calendar, looking to the future, and asking ourselves, 'Am I equipping her to make decisions for when she leaves the house?' we realized we weren't. We were doing what you warned us about. We were making every decision for her."

"So what did you do?"

"We basically admitted to her that it wasn't that we didn't want her to have a phone. It's just that we wanted her to learn to become wise with a phone. Then we took your advice and gave her a choice. We told her she could wait until she turned eighteen to get a phone, or she could start meeting with us once a week and go through your *Teen's Guide to Social Media* book with us, and then we'd give her a phone."

"So how long did it take?"

"We went through a few chapters a week, basically at her pace, discussing everything from what you're posting to who you're friending and how screens affect self-esteem." He choked up a little. "Best conversations we've ever had. Thank you."

You probably have this sentence memorized by now: parental controls can be helpful, *when partnered with open communication.*

## Discussion Questions

1. Why do you think focusing *too much* on parental controls can hinder the ability to engage your kids in meaningful dialogue?

2. How do screen guidelines, such as no phones in the bedroom, making sure kids are close by when watching screens, and waiting until high school to give your kids phones (to name just a few), lessen the need for an overabundance of parental controls?

3. Why is it helpful to require a parental password for your kids to download or delete apps?

4. Have you tried any content restrictions on your kids' devices, your Netflix accounts, or other features or apps? How did that work?

5. How would app limits help your kids with their social media intake? Are these limits foolproof? So what else can you do? (Hint: It's not a parental control; it's a conversation.)

6. Jonathan shared that the best porn blocker is engaging your kids in conversations (not just one conversation) about God's design for sex and intimacy. Is he right? Explain.

7. How can you begin pairing parental controls with open communication this week?

## CHAPTER 9

# When They Break the Rules

*Correcting without destroying connection*

I THOUGHT MY KIDS were all on board. We had talked about being screen-wise countless times. They knew exactly what was off-limits, but my son decided to cross the line anyway.

I can clearly remember the day it happened. I wasn't even snooping through his stuff. I just stumbled upon it. My son had downloaded some inappropriate music. Come to find out, he had downloaded it months earlier and was listening to it regularly.

I was hurt.

And when he got home, I let him know. He argued . . . and I blew up.

"Don't *even* argue with me," I yelled. "You know you weren't supposed to do this, yet you did."

He argued more, and the battle grew heated.

Lori came into the room and put her hand on my shoulder, simply saying, "Jonathan?" She was really saying, "Jonathan, do you realize you are out of control and need to stop now?"

But I turned to her and told her something idiotic. I said, "I got this." I lowered my voice for about ten seconds, until my son argued again, and then I blew up some more.

True story.

The part I remember most clearly is when my youngest daughter, Ashley, began crying. It tugged at my heart.

"Ashley, what's wrong?" I asked.

I'll never forget her words.

Between sniffles she simply said, "I'm just sad."

"Why?" I asked.

"Because you're being so mean."

It wasn't wrong to correct my son. He needed to be corrected. But the truth of the matter was, *I wasn't ready* to correct him at that moment.

I was out of control. "I got this" was the furthest thing from the truth. I didn't *have* anything. The only thing I ended up doing was shaming my son in front of the whole family, and the unintended result of that moment and others like it was that I clearly communicated to all three of my kids, *Dad isn't safe.*

## Safe

I hear it after every school assembly I speak at.

Kids come up to me and begin asking questions about sensitive subjects. I always respond the same way, almost as an experiment just to see how they'll respond. I ask them, "Have you tried talking with your parents about this?"

Students literally laugh and say, "There's no way I'd talk to them about this."

I ask, "Why?" and it's the same response every time.

"Because they'd freak out."

It's not that I'm some unique parent whom kids feel they can trust. Whenever I speak at a school assembly, I have two advantages:

1. I'm a stranger. The stranger-on-the-train phenomenon, as some psychologists call it, is when people find it easier to share something personal or vulnerable with someone they know they will never see again. The risk is minimal.

2. The kids just heard me talk about the issues at hand, and whenever I talk with students, I try to come across as someone who refrains from judgment and just provides them with good information so they can make an informed decision. This makes me seem safe.

There's that word again: *safe.*

It's a word I've been hearing in mental-health arenas a lot lately. When people feel safe, they'll open up and engage in meaningful conversation. When they feel shut down or shamed, they retreat.

How do your kids feel in your home?

Let me be clear. I'm not saying you shouldn't correct your kids. Just like they need loving limits, they need caring correction. But if you're like me, you might need a little work on the whole *caring* part of that correction. If we correct without care, our kids might resent our rebuke. And resentment leads to rebellion.

So how can you correct without shaming?

How can you correct in a way that makes your kids think about what they did and learn from their mistakes?

What can you do to help them

> *If we correct without care, our kids might resent our rebuke. And resentment leads to rebellion.*

feel safe with you? When they feel safe, they'll think, *Mom and Dad love me unconditionally. They're always there for me, even when I mess up.*

## Seven Tips for Correcting without Destroying Connection

Following are seven helpful tips that not only keep you from destroying connection but also catalyze connection. I wish I had learned these a little earlier in my parenting.

### 1. Prepare Yourself.

Your kids are going to break your rules. Prepare yourself for that moment.

Do you remember what it's like to be a teenager? All those insecurities, feelings, and desires bouncing around in your rapidly changing body?

It's even more sobering when we consider this fact: we have no idea what it's like to be a teenager today. Screens have provided some fun and convenience, but they have also added a lot of complexity to an already difficult time in young people's lives. The pressure screens are creating is like nothing any of us experienced when we were our children's age.

Let's say your twelve-year-old daughter, Jordan, already has a phone in middle school but desperately wants Instagram. You tell her, "Sorry. You can't do what all your friends are doing." You may say this without even considering what it's like when every other middle school kid is talking about what they saw on Instagram and your kid is out of the loop. Why is she out of the loop? Because she isn't allowed to have Instagram like her friends. Of course, she doesn't see the problem that way. She just hears other kids laughing and saying, "Oh right. Jordan's mommy doesn't let her have Instagram because it's evil."

So Jordan breaks the rules and downloads Instagram on her phone. It happens.

Even the kindest, most well-behaved, conscientious kids will mess up in some way. Maybe it will be something small . . . or it might be a whopper!

Are you ready for that moment?

Repeat after me: "My kids are going to break my rules."

Go ahead. Say it out loud right now. (Yes, if other people are in the room, they'll probably look at you funny. My dog looked up at me when I said it.)

It's going to happen. So prepare yourself for that moment. You're going to be hurt. You're going to take it personally. And if you're human, you might even be tempted to snap at your kid in anger.

That's why the next tip is the most important one.

## 2. Buy Yourself Some Time.

Even if you're the most self-controlled parent in the galaxy, giving yourself some time before responding to your child never hurts.

Most of us aren't at our best when we're put on the spot. And that's a great way to describe the exact moment you discover that one of your kids broke the rules. It won't be at the perfect time. It will catch you off guard, and you'll be put to the test right then and there—on the spot.

Your reaction matters.

Your kids will remember your reaction.

Your kids will consider this reaction one day in the future when they are feeling sad, lonely, or guilty and the thought pops into their heads, *Should I talk to Mom about this? Is Mom safe?*

What will they decide?

I'm not implying that if you lose your cool once, you've blown it, and your kids are now going to start selling drugs. Parents make mistakes, and it's okay for you to humbly apologize when you mess up. But if Mom or Dad overreacts all the time, your kids will begin to realize that you aren't safe.

Do your kids feel safe messing up?

Your kids don't need (or necessarily even want) a parent who lets them do anything they want. What they do need is a parent who is willing to listen and try to understand, a parent who doesn't freak out every time they mess up. *They need someone safe.*

Your on-the-spot responses influence this feeling of safety. So buy yourself some time. In fact, practice your response. Practice it now so you aren't searching for words in a moment of hurt and anger.

Maybe you can say something like this to your daughter:

> Wow. I don't even know what to say at this moment other than
> I love you so much, even when you break the rules. I need
> some time to think about this so I don't say something stupid.
> Please leave your phone on the kitchen table and go up to your
> room and do your homework. I need to pray.

Tone and volume are also vitally important. So take a breath before you say your rehearsed speech. Then say it calmly and softly.

*Safely.*

Do exactly what you told your kid you'd do: pray.

### 3. Admit, "I Don't Have This."

Pray and humble yourself before God. I say *humble yourself* because it's important in this moment to gain proper perspective. Point of fact, we all mess up, and none of us deserve any mercy. But God loves us so much that He has given us mercy at a huge price, the blood of His Son, Jesus. Jesus is *grace* and *mercy* wrapped into one. He's grace in that He is a gift we don't deserve. He's mercy in that through faith in Him, we are shown mercy and are saved from a punishment we do deserve. Our response to these amazing gifts should be humility (and probably a little bit of awe).

Humility is being wise enough to recognize the foolishness of the little voice in our heads that pridefully proclaims, *I got this! I don't need anyone's help!* Humility is remembering how flawed we are, enough to say, "I don't have this. In fact, God, I need Your love, mercy, and strength."

The cool thing about humbling ourselves and receiving God's mercy is that it tends to overflow. The more we open ourselves to it, the more it flows out of us. It's not something we even need to try to do; it's something we just allow Him to do in us.

So pray, confess your own imperfections to God, humble yourself before Him, and soak in His love, mercy, patience, kindness, and every other characteristic of love listed in 1 Corinthians 13.

Take hours if you need to.

Sleep on it if needed. Of course, let your kids out of their rooms after a couple of hours and tell them, "We're *not* going to talk about this today. I want to sleep on it and pray some more."

In fact, the waiting is a great punishment in itself. Your kids will *hate* it. They want to know, "What are you going to do?"

Don't even humor the notion. Tell them you need until tomorrow.

### 4. Ask Your Kids Their Side of the Story.

Let's get back to the situation with Jordan. When you're ready, sit down with her and say, "Let's talk about this." Quickly explain, literally in a sentence or two, what you observed.

"We made it clear that you weren't supposed to download Instagram until you turn thirteen. Yesterday I found this Instagram account on your phone, and it looks like you created this behind our backs."

Here's where you refrain from doing what many parents do: lecturing, jumping to conclusions, and imposing punishment without knowing the whole situation.

First, give your daughter a chance to be heard. Say, "I don't want to jump to any conclusions, so please tell us your side of the story. Did you do this? If so, please explain."

One of the biggest needs of young people today is to feel noticed and heard. Many kids feel their parents ignore—and *misunderstand*—them. Times like these are excellent opportunities to make your kids feel heard and understood.

> **One of the biggest needs of young people today is to feel noticed and heard.**

So listen when they talk. Here's a trick I've learned . . .

### 5. Secretly Become Your Kids' Defense Attorney.

I've repeated a word intentionally throughout this book that can change your relationship with your children. That word is *empathy*.

It's part of the five steps (six, actually) that we've repeated chapter after chapter to help you listen to your kids' points of view and create a climate of comfortable conversation in your home.

When your kids mess up and break the rules, you need to ask them their side of the story and step into their shoes. But it's much more difficult in these moments, because our tendency as parents is to shoot down their feeble excuses instead of seeking to understand. That's why when my kids were younger, I played a little game without their knowledge. Whenever I asked them to share their stories, I secretly became their defense attorney and began trying to build their case in my mind. This helped me try to see the situation from their perspective and figure out what the other side (which also happened to be me) needed to understand.

This can be eye opening.

No, I'm not some wishy-washy parent who lets my kids get away with everything. If they violate a rule, there will be consequences. I just want to get to the *why*, because in many cases, that exposes an even deeper problem or need that could be more important than the small infraction at hand.

Let's say your daughter says, "I don't know. I guess I just wanted Instagram. All my friends have it, and it feels like I'm the only one who doesn't. Christina and Lindsey made fun of me, so I just downloaded it."

Instead of jumping to correction, explore a little more by asking another question: "How was it?"

"I don't know," she replies. "Fun at first. But I don't have many followers. I'm not that pretty. People just don't like me."

Which is more important right now: your daughter's poor self-esteem or her sneaking behind your back to download Instagram?

I'm not in any way implying that disobeying is "no big deal" or that it shouldn't be corrected. It should. But your daughter's self-esteem is a much bigger deal. She probably doesn't even realize it, but some of these feelings of low self-esteem might have increased since she started using social media. If you read about the unintended effects of social media in chapter 5, you know that self-esteem issues are common with young girls who pin their hopes of being accepted on the screens in their pockets.

Now you have an amazing opportunity to talk with your daughter about her self-esteem. Think about that for a moment. Most parents would love an opportunity to dialogue with their daughters about their sense of self. But most girls aren't very responsive to Mom walking into their rooms and asking, "So how do you feel about yourself?"

I can imagine the response. "What? Get out!"

But in that moment, right after you've caught your daughter using the off-limits app, she would much rather talk about her feelings in hopes that you'll understand and show her mercy.

Read that again: *in hopes that you'll understand.*

That's really what she wants.

So in this case, listen and talk about her self-esteem. Maybe even ask her, "What if we went out for frozen yogurt one day a week after school and talked about this?"

My daughter Alyssa wrote a book for teenagers with me, *The Teen's Guide to Face-to-Face Connections in a Screen-to-Screen World*. In that book she tells about a particular day when she posted a bunch of pics with friends, and after looking at them, she thought, *Are my arms really that big?* and *Why do I look like Jabba the Hutt all of a sudden?* Later at home, she saw the stories her friends had posted on Instagram and realized that she wasn't in a single photo. She confesses that she ended up sobbing on her bed, at age twenty-four. That's the day she decided to take a break from Instagram and all the pressure of comparing herself with others.

Wouldn't it be cool to open up the dialogue about these issues with your daughter?

## 6. Ask Your Kids What They'd Do in Your Shoes.

But what about breaking the rules? Does poor self-esteem excuse bad behavior?

Here's another great opportunity to turn situations like these into valuable teaching moments. For instance, if your daughter downloaded Instagram without your permission, ask her this question: "What would you do if *your* daughter did this? What would be a fair response to teach her that sneaking behind your back isn't okay?"

See what your daughter comes up with. Who knows, it might be something even better than whatever you had in mind.

Compliment her for her ideas and thoughts.

## 7. Give Your Kids a Choice.

In our hypothetical example, your daughter broke the rules by downloading Instagram on her phone because she felt it would help her fit in and feel affirmed by her friends. In a moment when she's already feeling powerless and a little bit ashamed (which is different than shamed), give her some power. Give her a choice. Talk it over with your spouse ahead of time, making sure you both agree on the choice, and then present it to your child.

You might say, "Okay, I'm going to let you choose your consequences. You can do one of two things:

"One: you lose your phone for a month and delete Instagram.

"Or two: you keep your phone, limit Instagram to only twenty minutes a day, and agree to meeting together every week to read through a book on social media and self-esteem so you can learn how to balance these feelings yourself."

Which option would your daughter choose?

As a parent you're going to encounter countless situations that allow you to give your kids a choice. In these moments, try to come up with one option that includes very heavy rules and limits and another option with much lighter rules and limits combined with a weekly time of connection.

Your kids are going to mess up. When they do, you have the opportunity to turn it into a teaching moment.

And guess what?

Sometimes after all of these steps, your twelve-year-old daughter will still complain, "But Mom, all my friends have Instagram! What's the big deal? You're so unfair!"

That's when you just have to say, "Nevertheless . . . "

My good friend Jim Burns, author of countless parenting books, taught me that. Sometimes there is nothing you can do. Your kids aren't going to agree with you no matter what. Life isn't fair, and that's okay.

So you say, "Nevertheless . . . you still can't lie about your age to get Instagram."

But don't jump straight to responding with *nevertheless*. Start with the seven tips we just discussed. These tips give your kids a chance to feel noticed and heard. The seven tips also give them an opportunity to think through what they've done and empower them to choose what happens next.

Practice "the Seven":

1. *Prepare yourself.* Your kids are going to break your rules, and you're going to be tempted to overreact.

2. *Buy yourself some time.* Practice a response where you tell your kids you love them unconditionally and you admit you need some time to think and pray about the situation. Be someone safe whom your kids can turn to when they mess up, because they know you won't freak out.

3. *Admit, "I don't have this."* Pray and humble yourself before God. Ask Him for patience. Take hours if you need to. Let God's love fill you so it overflows to your kids.

4. *Ask your kids their side of the story.* Listen to them. Give them a chance to be heard, noticed, and understood.

5. *Secretly become your kids' defense attorney.* Empathize with your kids. Step into their shoes and try to see the situation from their perspective. Seek to understand their side of the story.

6. *Ask your kids what they'd do in your shoes.* Turn the situation into a valuable teaching moment. Give your kids the opportunity to step into your shoes as a parent and consider how a loving mom or dad should respond in the situation.

7. *Give your kids a choice.* Come up with one option that includes very heavy rules and limits and another option with much lighter

rules and limits combined with a weekly time of connection. Let your child choose one of these options.

Correction doesn't need to destroy connection.

Do your kids feel safe to fail?

## Discussion Questions

1. Share a time when you corrected your kids even though you weren't ready to do so.

2. Which of Jonathan's seven tips for correcting without destroying connection do you need most?

3. How come most of us don't practice the simple habit of pausing the conversation until we've had time to think and pray?

4. Jonathan confessed his need to stop, pray for humility, and rely on God's strength for these tough moments of correction. Honestly, have you ever tried that? Do you need to?

   Read Ephesians 6:4. What do you think this passage is telling parents? How does that apply to moments of correction?

5. What do you think of Jonathan's advice to not only give your kids a chance to share their side of the story but also secretly become their defense attorney? How might that change your perspective?

6. I know this is a tough question, but do your kids feel safe to fail?

## CHAPTER 10

# Putting It into Practice

*Real-world stories from moms and dads
parenting Generation Screen*

AT THE END OF EVERY ONE of my Parenting Generation Screen workshops, I always save time for moms and dads to ask me questions. I do my best to provide answers.

Some questions are fairly specific:

- "Jonathan, what about this new app that teenagers are downloading?"

- "Jonathan, have you seen that new Netflix show my kid says everyone is watching?"

- "Jonathan, I've tried setting parental controls on the new iPhone, but now they've made updates. Can you help me figure it out?"

One of the struggles we experience as we try to help our kids wisely navigate entertainment media is that *it's always changing.* The moment you think you understand your kid's favorite app, a new app emerges. The day after you set the parental controls on your kids' devices, an update is released, and you have to revisit those controls.

That's one of the reasons it's helpful to connect with other parents who are experiencing the same struggles you experience *today* as you parent Generation Screen. It's nice to know you aren't alone.

> ### It's nice to know you aren't alone.

When my kids were teens and tweens, my wife and I helped lead a Sunday morning fellowship group (dare I call it a Sunday school class?) at our church. It was appropriately named the Family Zone. Moms and dads from this unique life stage—they all had kids in middle school or high school—met together for encouragement, fellowship, and teaching. Each week a speaker would teach on faith, marriage, or parenting, and then we'd discuss it. I loved teaching this class because I knew I could easily kick off the discussion by providing a case study.

For example, I'd say, "Your sixteen-year-old son comes home and announces that he doesn't want to go to church anymore. He says, 'Church is stupid.' How do you respond?"

Or "Your daughter has been posting videos on YouTube, and today she tells you that she doesn't want to go to college anymore because she wants to be an influencer. What do you tell her?"

After sharing one of these situations, I'd walk around the tables and eavesdrop on the conversations. I can't tell you how many times I would hear, "Well, actually, Chris did come home and say that last summer." And another person in the group would share, "Taylor did the same thing."

Then I'd inevitably hear, "So what did you do?"

It's good to know someone else is going through the same thing, isn't it?

Chances are, many of you might be struggling with very specific issues like these:

- I'm a single mom with two kids, ages ten and twelve, and they already have phones. Their dad gave them phones last year, even though I told him we should wait.

- Our daughter is truly obsessed with social media. She's a good kid, but she is way too caught up with what others think of her. Social media has made this one hundred times worse.

- My wife and I didn't give our kids screens, but their school did. At school the devices have all sorts of content blockers, but we learned the hard way that those devices didn't have those blockers when on our home network.

- Our kids are grown and out of the house, but now our youngest daughter, a twenty-four-year-old single mom, is struggling with personal issues, so we are helping her raise her kids in our home. It's really difficult because she lets them have anything they want.

- My husband and I homeschool our kids, now thirteen, fifteen, and sixteen, and they have limited access to screens. But recently, my sixteen-year-old spent the night at her friend's house, and the two of them watched . . .

- My son won't stop playing video games—ever! And when we do stop him, he throws a fit. Every time. He's intolerable.

Maybe you can relate to one or more of these scenarios.

After I finished writing this book, I gave my loyal readers an opportunity to review it as a work in progress. I asked them to please write comments, make suggestions, and share stories of how these issues played out in their homes. As I read many of these stories, I connected certain parents.

"You two should talk," I told them. "You're going through the exact same thing."

In fact, even some of the marketing people asked me, "What did you tell her? My daughter told me the same thing last month."

It quickly became obvious that many of these issues were painfully common, and parents were desperate to talk with other parents experiencing the same thing. They wanted to ask, "What did you do?" and "How did that work?"

For this reason, I'm going to share a few stories from other parents. Then I'll offer a little feedback—literally just a few sentences—at the end of each story.

Enjoy!

## YouTube Envy

Our son is eight years old, and he's already feeling the pressure to be on YouTube.

And we're not alone.

We became fast friends with four other couples at our church with kids the same age. Our families do a lot together, and the kids always have fun running around playing with each other.

Sadly, one of the couples already let their son—also eight years old—have his own phone. His favorite pastime is watching funny YouTube videos. Now, whenever all our kids are together, we always see him with his phone out and every other kid gathered around the phone laughing at some funny video.

This kid also has his own YouTube account, and he makes videos. All the other kids think it's cool and say, "Wow, you're on YouTube! Look how many likes you got on that one!"

But mostly, they just sit and watch videos.

I've watched some of the videos—they aren't bad. But we've begun to notice two things:

1. The kids don't want to run around and play as much as they used to. They just want to sit around and watch videos on this boy's phone.

2. All the other kids, including mine, want phones now so they can watch YouTube. They ask for our phones during every car ride, and they even want their own YouTube accounts like this boy's so they can get likes.

We don't want to hate on our friends, but we're all kind of bitter that they gave their kid a phone, because it's truly having an effect on our kids.

Anything we can do?

—Lyla

Thanks for sharing, Lyla. You're not alone. A favorite activity of young people today is watching funny online videos, and YouTube is the channel of choice. And it's nice when parents of young kids band together and agree, "Hey, let's not give our kids phones until they are at least thirteen." That makes it easier for all. But in your situation, show the one kid with the phone lots of grace and balance that with times of creative alternatives. Say, "Okay, everyone, enough screen time." Then suggest another option: "Let's all make cookies," or go on a hike, or make a couch-cushion fort, or do some other nonscreen activity.

—JONATHAN

## Weekend Binge

My wife and I were going away for a weekend and leaving our teens at home. We thought, *What could happen in just one weekend?*

*Oy vey!*

Our daughters, sixteen and eighteen, have always had the rule "No phones in the bedroom after 9:30 p.m." We charge the phones in our bedroom. Our sixteen-year-old actually thanked us for this recently—because it allows her to paint and do art and stuff. It also gives her an excuse to end conversations and avoid the social pressure, because she can say, "My parents make me put my phone away at 9:30."

My wife and I were going on a weekend trip, and we decided to leave our girls at home by themselves because they had earned our trust. We put our eighteen-year-old in charge and removed the screen-time restriction from our sixteen-year-old, who had argued that she needed to have twenty-four-hour access to us for emergencies in case her sister wasn't around. We agreed, because she's honestly an incredibly responsible teenager.

The weekend seemed to go well, but when we got home, our sixteen-year-old was acting peculiar. Nothing specific, just being overly nice and almost clingy. I was doing all I could not to ask, "Okay, what happened?"

That night she came into our room and started talking. She never does this. But soon she began confessing that she had a boyfriend, and she wondered if she could go on a date with him.

This was completely out of left field, because, literally, the prior weekend she had told us how much she was enjoying school, youth group, and her friends, and that she didn't even feel the need to date in high school.

It felt like we were talking to a different girl.

I was exhausted, so I said, "This is a lot to think about. Can we think about this and talk tomorrow?"

She agreed and went to bed.

As I crawled into bed, I couldn't stop thinking, *What happened?* Then I realized that her phone was right there, ten feet from where I was sleeping.

I've always reserved the right to look at her phone—I have her passwords, and I used to look a lot when she was younger. But I honestly hadn't done that in at least a year.

That night I looked.

Texts were normal.

Insta-posts were normal.

Snapchat. Who knows. (I hate that app.)

But then I remembered her Instagram DMs.

There it was!

Friday night she got into a long DM conversation with a boy I'd never met named Cody. They had started messaging after school, and the conversation kept going. It was mostly boring. "Yeah, I hate French class," "I've never been to another country," and so forth. Then I noticed that the conversation changed a bit. They started talking about dating in general. Then, "I really like you a lot," and soon, "I think we should date."

No nude photos, no inappropriate talk . . . but then I noticed the time.

2:17 a.m.

2:37 a.m.

2:57 a.m.

They had continued to talk until almost 3:00 in the morning and just stopped short of saying "I love you" to each other. All DMs, late at night when they were tired and caught up in emotion.

The next day, I asked my daughter, "So what time did you and Cody have that conversation about dating?"

The look on her face said it all. She immediately started making excuses. "I know we were talking late, and I should have gone to bed, but you guys were gone, and I just wasn't thinking . . . blah blah blah."

A day or two passed, and she wasn't that interested in this boy anymore, nor he in her. Apparently it was just a late-night emotional connection that neither really wanted once reality hit.

Since then, she's been a little more eager and willing to give us her phone at night. I feel as if she's almost saying, "Take this. I don't want to do anything stupid."

Next time, we're probably going to think twice about leaving the kids alone.

—Rick

Thanks for sharing, Rick. I can tell you twenty stories of stupid things I did when I was fifteen, sixteen, and seventeen years old, all when my parents were out of town. The good news is it sounds like your daughter learned from her experience. It's like I always say, "Most of us don't make good decisions after 11:00 p.m."

—JONATHAN

## Windshield Conversations

My sixteen-year-old and I have a rule for the car, especially driving to school: "Cars are for conversations." No screens, no radio, no headphones.

Me, too. I don't answer the phone when my son is in the car.

I'm glad he opted into this rule when he was young, because it's like he's never known anything different. So whenever I pick him up from school, he just starts talking. He knows it's *his* time. He likes that I listen.

Sometimes I don't say one single word the entire drive home, and then when he gets out of the car, he says, "Nice talking with you, Dad."

I've heard people say that men prefer not looking each other in the eyes when they talk. They talk more when they're looking forward doing something else. I have no idea if that's true. All I know is that when we're in the car . . . we talk.

No complaints.
—James

That's awesome, James. Many of us are jealous. I love that you established this rule when your son was young and built good habits. Good listeners are rare these days. Once your son got a taste of having his dad listen to him, he knew where he could always get it. Keep up the good work!

—JONATHAN

## Video Star

It has been four years since my daughter got her phone, and we have never had any problems at all—until now. After a lot of deliberation, I allowed her to start a TikTok account. I've never regretted anything more.

Two weeks in, we began noticing a change. She would disappear into her room; then we'd hear her singing songs, many with foul lyrics; and then she began dressing—how to even describe it—*more sexy*. Eventually I confronted her, and she didn't respond well.

Two more weeks passed, and we noticed more of the same. Again I talked with her. Nothing.

It's been five weeks now. I don't even recognize my little girl anymore. She's acting out and having outbursts. I can actually see physical symptoms of stress manifesting, so much so that I did something I've never done before. I peeked at her phone. I couldn't believe what I saw.

She was texting friends links to TikTok videos she had made. The lyrics and subject matter were horrifying.

So I'm at an impasse. She hasn't responded to any of my conversations. I'm wondering if I should limit social media, ban TikTok specifically, or take her phone away completely.

I just read your previous chapter about correcting without destroying connection. I'm going to try the seven tips today.

I'd love your prayers!
—Jessica

Thanks for sharing, Jessica. I wish I could tell you this was uncommon, but honestly, I'm not even surprised anymore when I hear stories like this, particularly when you consistently see the pressure social media is putting on young people, girls especially. I hope the seven tips help you connect. We're all praying for you as you continue to respond to your daughter in grace and truth.

—JONATHAN

## Data Hog

Last year my wife and I moved to a rural area without any decent internet connections. After almost a month of research, I finally found an internet provider that offered a decently reliable tiered plan with only so many gigabytes of data. After that's used, it drops to the next slower tier. Well, we didn't have a problem with it until my eighteen-year-old son moved back home.

He had been home just four days, when all of a sudden, our Netflix began streaming in extremely low res—with pixels the size of a pizza box. Come to find out, he had been gaming every night since he moved in. He used up a month's worth of high-speed internet in just three days.

Of course, when I asked him about it, he said, "What? That's stupid. Why don't you have fast internet?"

I tried to explain, but he wasn't interested in understanding.

The next month he did it again—using up the data allowance in two days. This time I didn't even say anything. I just changed the password. About ten o'clock that night, there was a knock on my bedroom door.

*Oh, you're ready to talk now, eh?* I thought.

—Robert

Ha. Well, Robert, you can certainly attest that parenting adult children is never easy. (I have three.) On paper, they're adults who can legally live on their own, but sometimes, mentally, they are still children lacking real-world experience of "adulting." Parenting adult children needs to be more about *coaching* than *parenting*. You can't tell your eighteen-year-old how to live his life. At the same time, that doesn't mean giving him whatever he wants. We have to balance the truth with smiling and telling our adult kids that we love them. In your case, that could mean saying, "Get your own internet, you data hog!"

—JONATHAN

## Foster Love

I'm a Court Appointed Special Advocate (CASA) volunteer who ensures that children and youth in the foster-care system have both a voice and the services they need for a stable future. I was matched with a family last year that's fostering three brothers, ages five, six, and eight. And boy, do these kids have a lot of energy.

The first time I picked these boys up to take them to swim lessons, they saw the big screen on the dash of my Subaru. All three yelled, "Wow, look at that screen!" And without any hesitation, they started punching buttons.

It took me an hour just to undo what they had done.

The first time I pulled out my phone to write down a date in my calendar, they did the same thing.

"Cool! An iPhone. Can I see it? Pleeeeease!" And they wouldn't let up about it.

Bottom line: *These kids love screens!*

Every time I'm with them, they're begging to play with a screen.

One time when I took a picture of them, they all began asking, "Can I see it? Pleeeeese?" I got tired of saying no, so next time I took a photo, I asked them, "Do you want to see it?"

"Yes! Yes! Yes!"

So I showed them not only the picture I just took, but my other pictures as well.

Soon, they started asking me questions about my photos. "Is that your dog? What's his name? What kind of dog is he?"

And that led me to ask them, "Do you have a dog? What kind? What's your favorite pet? Do you take care of him? Are you going to have a pet when you grow up? What kind?"

I quickly realized something: pictures create conversation.

Now I'm taking a lot more photos.

—Tim

You're a good man, Tim. Today's young people need positive mentors desperately. Thanks for helping out young people in the foster-care system. And I'm so glad you discovered a way to use screens to catalyze conversations. Nice tip.

—JONATHAN

## Saying Yes

Have you ever noticed how often parents say no?

Maybe it was just me, but I began noticing that I was saying no to my kids half a dozen times a day.

"Dad, can I watch TV?"

"No."

"Dad, can I have some ice cream?"

"No."

"Dad, can I stay up and play video games?"

"No."

I got tired of being the bad guy. So I began rewording my answers so my kids heard yes more than no.

For example, if I was talking with my wife and my kids interrupted, instead of saying, "I can't talk right now," I said, "I'd love to talk with you as soon as I'm done talking with Mommy."

Or if one of my kids asked me, "Dad, can I go over to my friend's house on a school night?" instead of saying, "No. Go to bed!" I would say, "You definitely can go to your friend's on the weekend sometime. Or maybe you would like to have your friend over this weekend?"

This took a lot of practice, but I noticed my kids felt less shut down.

—George

Thanks, George. That's solid advice. This is a great way to focus on connection more than correction. Keep up the good work.

—JONATHAN

## Distance Learning?

It seemed like screens in our home were under control until last year when our country shut everything down. We barely left the house anymore, and my son had to do distance learning.

Without any of his normal activities, my eight-year-old turned to screens. This required a lot more attention from my husband and me because we didn't know anything about half the games he wanted to play.

After reading a PluggedIn.com review of one of his games, we blocked it. But this didn't stop him from going on YouTube and watching videos of other kids playing it. We began noticing him using some swear words and discovered he was learning them from these videos. (YouTube definitely isn't for eight-year-olds.) This became really difficult to monitor. He was supposed to be doing schoolwork, but he would switch over to YouTube. We tried setting some parental controls, but he got around them. So we tried to be in the room whenever he was distance-learning on his screen. But do you realize how much time that is each day? That's a lot of time being in the room. And honestly, sometimes we can't even tell the difference between his online math games and other games.

I hate screens!

—Alyssa

Thanks, Alyssa. You're not the only one frustrated with distance learning. We want our kids to have unlimited access to learning, but it's tricky to keep that from becoming unlimited access to everything else. Sigh. One thing you can do is simply block YouTube completely from his devices. I agree with you: YouTube is definitely not for eight-year-olds. So block it completely.

—JONATHAN

## Alone

I could relate when Jonathan wrote about that group of middle school kids who all had phones—every single one of them.

My twelve-year-old son (almost thirteen) is truly the only one of his friends at school who doesn't have a phone.

This year, none of his close friends had the same classes as he did, but he was positive about it, saying he could at least find his friends to sit and talk with at lunch. After a week or so, I asked him if he was at least enjoying getting to talk with his friends at lunch, and with a disappointed look on his face, he said, "Not really."

When I asked him why, he said, "Everyone was on their phone the whole time." That was how I learned that all his classmates had phones, and they were allowed to have them out during lunch with no restrictions.

Jonathan's right. The pressure is on. It's been so hard *not* getting my son a phone. My wife and I are definitely getting him one when he turns thirteen in a few months. We're actually going through one of Jonathan's *Teen's Guide* books now to prep him for the responsibility.

—Jake

Thanks, Jake. The struggle is real. The world is putting the pressure on kids to own screens at a ridiculously young age. Glad you're prepping your son for the responsibility. Let me know if those discussion questions at the end of each chapter in my *Teen's Guide* book are helpful.

—JONATHAN

## Screen Sneaks

My kids gravitate toward screens. Block one, and they'll find another.

The other day my kids had been watching TV for a while, so I told them they'd had enough screens for now. After about two hours of housework, I noticed my eleven-year-old was MIA. I went looking around for her and found her hiding in the basement playing Roblox on one of our old phones. (We didn't even know the phone still existed.) I took away the phone and talked to her about the sneaking around—not cool. And then that night, I kid you not, I went into her room to find her under the covers playing the same game on her laptop.

I didn't react very well.

How many screens does this house have?

*The world is putting the pressure on kids to own screens at a ridiculously young age.*

Sadly, she's not alone. I've caught her older sister on her phone at one o'clock and two o'clock in the morning several times. We take away our kids' screens, and then when they get them back, the problems happen again.

I'm finding myself being reactive. This book is nudging me to become a little more proactive. Thanks for the advice!

—Lindsey

Lindsey, I'm so sorry to hear about your kids pushing the limits. That's not easy to navigate. But I encourage you to do exactly as you wrote—become more proactive. Talk with your girls about the reasoning behind the rules. Don't just take screens away. Teach them why you don't want them on screens at 1:00 a.m. Help them understand so they'll be equipped to make these decisions on their own.

—JONATHAN

## Connection before Correction

My daughter Willow has been on her screen a little more than usual these days. Normally she's shown amazing responsibility. But every once in a while, she needs a reminder to look up from that distracting little device and enjoy the world around her.

Last week I decided to talk with her, and having just read your book, I thought I'd try your five steps of connection before correction. After all, they looked pretty good on paper.

So I did exactly what you said. When I found a particularly informative part of the book, I sat down with her and shared some of the eye-opening data you mentioned. Then I asked her what she thought, and it was a fascinating discussion.

She then assured me, "Dad, I'm not like all the other kids out there on their phones." I couldn't help but wonder, *Was she assuring me? Or herself?*

I agreed with her. And that conversation opened up even more discussions.

One of the biggest challenges for her is not having the phone in her bedroom. It's like you said. "Dad, aaaaall of my friends have phones in their bedrooms."

So I'm not laying down the law. It's still an open discussion. But overall I've been very pleased with her attitude about her phone.

—Joel

Joel, Willow sounds like an amazing girl. It sounds like you have truly created a climate of comfortable conversation in your home. Keep up the good work. (And as our friend Jim Burns says, "Nevertheless," pull that phone out of the bedroom.)

—JONATHAN

## Obsessed

Our sixth-grade daughter received a smartphone for her birthday last year. We thought it was a wise idea, since she started playing volleyball and we figured she could text us when practice was over.

Little did we know that our sweet girl would become *obsessed* with that phone, and any request to put it away would be torture!

She is not allowed on social media, but apps like YouTube and Roblox consume her! Gone are the days of her jumping on her trampoline or swimming in her pool!

Parents, don't make the same mistake we did!

—Kelly

Kelly, I can't really argue with you. I agree. Hindsight is twenty-twenty. Thanks for your vulnerability and admitting you'd rethink that decision. I agree that sixth grade is a little early to give kids a phone. But you can't squeeze the toothpaste back in the tube. So try what I recommended earlier in the book. Lobotomize that phone to the max and seek out points of connection with your daughter so she experiences the joy of face-to-face contact in a screen-to-screen world.

—JONATHAN

## Discussion Questions

1. Which of these parenting stories did you identify with the most? Why?

2. Which story did you need to hear most? Why?

3. What parenting story would you share with Jonathan? What makes your story similar to or different from the stories in this chapter?

4. As you consider the stories in this chapter, which of your parenting practices may you need to adjust?

5. How can you avoid overreacting with your children when you hear stories about other kids acting out?

6. How can other people pray for you as you parent Generation Screen?

7. How can others help you?

## CHAPTER 11

# Time for Pizza

*Sharing your plan for becoming a screenwise family*

IT'S TIME.

Throughout this book, I've been repeating my advice: *Delay correction and decisions. Actually walk away. Don't rush to set boundaries or impose a decision right away. Tell your kids you need some time to think and pray about the situation.*

Delaying can be tough. I know my personality wants to *solve this problem right now!* I don't want to wait. But solving screen-related issues isn't a feat that any parent can accomplish in one night. As I've said throughout the book, the first step to solving this issue is to listen to your kids and make them feel noticed, heard, and loved.

If you've tried that—listening, noticing, validating, being thoughtful, being present—you've paved the way for this pizza meeting where reasonable rules are discussed. If you do the "hard time" of listening to your kids and making them feel understood, they're going to respect your rules far more than if they see you as some cold, distant authoritarian.

*Connection* paves the way for *correction.*

So if you've tried the five steps laid out in this book, you've already been creating a climate of comfortable conversation in your home. Specifically, you've done the following:

1. Set up a family gathering, opening the door for dialogue by asking fun questions to help your kids feel safe sharing.

2. Brought up issues about your kids' screens by reading a noteworthy paragraph or study from this book, asking your kids' opinions, and then listening and asking questions instead of lecturing.

3. Practiced empathy by stepping into your kids' shoes and trying to understand their viewpoints and feelings without criticizing their responses.

4. Asked your kids, "What do you think is best? How would you solve the problem at hand?"

5. Delayed correction or decisions, taking time to think and pray about the situation rather than rushing to set boundaries or impose a decision right away.

You may even have begun connecting with your kids regularly to talk about becoming screenwise, read a book together, and have a dialogue about what you read. This can be helpful because young people are often more open to changing some of their habits if they hear advice from an expert outside the home.

But eventually you, the parent, have to make some decisions. You have to answer the big questions your kids are asking:

"Can I have a phone? All my friends have one."

"Why can't I have my phone in my bedroom? It's my alarm clock."

"Why do you care so much about how much time I spend playing my video games? I'm going to earn money doing this someday!"

"What's the harm in watching a bunch of stupid YouTube videos? They're no big deal."

It's time to set a date to actually talk with your kids about what you've read in this book and make some final decisions about screens.

Give your kids advance notice: "This Thursday we're going out for pizza to talk about how we can become screenwise in this house."

Here's where you lay out the plan. And the best advice I can give is this: keep it simple. I've seen some pretty detailed screen contracts with thirty rules and specific consequences for each rule. I'm not knocking these contracts; they're just a lot to remember *and a lot to enforce.* Don't set up yourself (and your kids) for failure.

The screen limits you give your kids will vary by age. If you have younger kids, you'll want to be more strict and allow less screen time. The biggest bomb you'll drop on younger kids is this: "No phones or social media until you're thirteen or fourteen *and* until you've read a book about becoming screenwise. Remember, you can't drive a car until you've read the manual and taken the driving test."

If you have adolescents, you need to remember they're beginning to discover their independence. That's actually a good thing, because you don't want them unemployed and living in your basement when they're thirty. So with teens, you'll have simpler rules, along with opportunities for your kids to earn your trust. Maybe you'll let your fifteen-year-old have Instagram even if you don't like it. Choose your battles.

Maybe you'll pull some of your guidelines right out of chapter 6, where I recommended screen-time guidelines for various age groups. Let's say your kids are already teenagers (thirteen or older) and have their own devices. Your rules for your teens might look something like this:

1. Don't bring your devices into the bedroom at night. Period.

2. Turn off your screens one hour before bedtime.

3. Limit social media to just one or two hours per day.

4. Set your social media profiles to *private*—even if you want to be an influencer. (Maybe consider letting sixteen- or seventeen-year-olds have more freedom in this area so they learn how to recognize predatory behaviors and navigate this dangerous landscape before they're out on their own.)

5. Respect no-tech zones, such as at the dinner table or in designated reading areas.

6. Don't wear headphones in the house.

That's only six rules. Not bad. Avoid adding more rules or screen limits unless your kids' behaviors begin to spiral out of control. They will be thrilled with just six rules. Simply tell them, "If we notice other screen activities hurting relationships, grades, or exercise, we'll add some more reasonable screen limits to help you maintain a healthy balance."

You might even ask your kids, "What do you think these out-of-balance behaviors might look like?" This will help them think through behaviors they want to avoid, such as playing video games for ten hours straight.

Once you've established the rules, you can also set parental controls to filter content. Make use of the age ratings on Netflix as well as the content filters on phones and computers. But remember: the filters aren't rules.

If your kids resist any of these limits, remember the advice about presenting them with a choice between two alternatives. This gives your kids an opportunity to prove themselves. For example, if you choose to limit social media to one hour, and your daughter strenuously objects, consider offering her this choice:

> Well, what would you rather do? We can keep the limit to just one hour a day, or I can increase the limit to ninety minutes a day, and you and I can continue meeting weekly like we did when you first got your phone. This time we'll go through a new book together.

No matter which rules you decide on, remember to keep the door open for dialogue. No, this doesn't mean letting your kids have their way. If they totally disagree with your rules, the only thing left to say will be "Nevertheless, these are the rules."

But your conversations will pave the way toward making this screenwise road a little easier. Your investment in listening, empathizing, validating, and just being present in your children's lives will make this pizza gathering less painful.

*No matter which rules you decide on, remember to keep the door open for dialogue.*

*Connection before correction.*
*Love before limits.*
*Bonding before boundaries.*

Screens have undeniably made parenting more difficult. But your love, patience, God-given humility, and continued efforts to seek parenting wisdom from others will certainly help you equip your kids to become screenwise as they discover their own independence. After all, you eventually have to "throw them the keys."

Are you preparing them for that day?

## Discussion Questions

1. Where is your favorite place to get pizza? (Let's be honest, pizza is manna from heaven!)

2. Throughout the book, Jonathan encouraged you to delay this pizza "meeting," when you finally sit down with your kids and present screen expectations for your home. What are some of the expectations or rules you think you'll lay out at that gathering?

3. What is one rule you think your kids might struggle with most?

4. What is one rule you're unsure about?

5. How are you going to begin your family meeting?

6. How are you going to end it?

7. How are you going to adjust these rules as your kids get older, so they'll be ready to leave home?

# Notes

**CHAPTER 1: THEY DON'T TELL YOU THIS STUFF**

1. Victoria Rideout and Michael B. Robb, *The Common Sense Census: Media Use by Teens and Tweens, 2019* (San Francisco: Common Sense Media, 2019), 5, https://www.commonsensemedia.org/sites/default/files/uploads/research/2019 -census-8-to-18-full-report-updated.pdf.

2. "Social Media, Social Life: Teens Reveal Their Experiences," Common Sense Media, September 10, 2018, https://www.commonsensemedia.org/social-media -social-life-infographic.

3. From survey conducted March 7–April 10, 2018, in Monica Anderson and Jingjing Jiang, *Teens, Social Media and Technology 2018* (Washington, DC: Pew Research Center, 2018), 2, https://www.pewresearch.org/internet/2018/05/31 /teens-social-media-technology-2018/.

4. Morning Consult, *The Influencer Report: Engaging Gen Z and Millennials*, cited in Sarah Min, "86% of Young Americans Want to Become a Social Media Influencer," CBS News, November 8, 2019, https://www.cbsnews.com/news /social-media-influencers-86-of-young-americans-want-to-become-one.

5. Jean M. Twenge, "Have Smartphones Destroyed a Generation?," *Atlantic*, September 2017, https://www.theatlantic.com/magazine/archive/2017/09/has -the-smartphone-destroyed-a-generation/534198/.

6. Rideout and Robb, *The Common Sense Census*, 3.

7. Michael B. Robb, *Screens and Sleep: The New Normal; Parents, Teens, Screens, and Sleep in the United States* (San Francisco, Common Sense Media, 2019), 26, https://www.commonsensemedia.org/sites/default/files/uploads/research/2019 -new-normal-parents-teens-screens-and-sleep-united-states-report.pdf.

**CHAPTER 2: CONNECTION BEFORE CORRECTION**

1. Candice L. Odgers and Michael B. Robb, *Tweens, Teens, Tech, and Mental Health: Coming of Age in an Increasingly Digital, Uncertain, and Unequal World 2020* (San Francisco: Common Sense Media, 2020), 13, https://www.commonsensemedia .org/sites/default/files/uploads/pdfs/tweens-teens-tech-and-mental-health-full -report-final-for-web1.pdf.

## CHAPTER 3: WHAT AGE?

1. "Social Media, Social Life: Teens Reveal Their Experiences," Common Sense Media, September 10, 2018, https://www.commonsensemedia.org/social-media -social-life-infographic.
2. Emily Retter, "Billionaire Tech Mogul Bill Gates Reveals He Banned His Children from Mobile Phones until They Turned 14," *Mirror*, April 21, 2017, https://www.mirror.co.uk/tech/billionaire-tech-mogul-bill-gates-10265298.
3. Brian X. Chen, "What's the Right Age for a Child to Get a Smartphone?," *New York Times*, July 20, 2016, https://www.nytimes.com/2016/07/21/technology /personaltech/whats-the-right-age-to-give-a-child-a-smartphone.html.
4. Greg Lukianoff, Adam Goldstein, and Pamela Paresky, "Catching Up with 'Coddling' Part Two: Trigger Warnings, Screen Time v. Social Media, COVID-19 and the Continuing Decline of Gen Z's Mental Health," FIRE, May 12, 2020, https://www.thefire.org/catching-up-with-coddling-part-two-trigger-warnings -screen-time-v-social-media-covid-19-and-the-continuing-decline-of-gen-zs -mental-health/.
5. Chen, "What's the Right Age?"
6. Chen, "What's the Right Age?"
7. Simon Sinek, *This Addiction Is Ruining the Upcoming Generation* (YouTube video), InnerLight Media, December 13, 2018.
8. Tristan Harris, interview by Christophe Haubursin in *It's Not You. Phones Are Designed to Be Addicting* (video), Vox, February 27, 2018, https://www.vox.com /2018/2/27/17053758/phone-addictive-design-google-apple.
9. Candice L. Odgers and Michael B. Robb, *Tweens, Teens, Tech, and Mental Health: Coming of Age in an Increasingly Digital, Uncertain, and Unequal World 2020* (San Francisco: Common Sense Media, 2020), 13, https://www.commonsensemedia .org/sites/default/files/uploads/pdfs/tweens-teens-tech-and-mental-health-full -report-final-for-web1.pdf.
10. Federal Trade Commission, "Children's Online Privacy Protection Rule ('COPPA')," 16 CFR Part 312, https://www.ftc.gov/enforcement/rules/rulemaking-regulatory -reform-proceedings/childrens-online-privacy-protection-rule; see also Federal Trade Commission, "Complying with COPPA: Frequently Asked Questions, https:// www.ftc.gov/tips-advice/business-center/guidance/complying-coppa-frequently -asked-questions-0.
11. Nellie Bowles, "A Dark Consensus about Screens and Kids Begins to Emerge in Silicon Valley," *New York Times*, October 26, 2018, https://www.nytimes.com /2018/10/26/style/phones-children-silicon-valley.html.
12. Bowles, "A Dark Consensus."

## CHAPTER 4: "MOM, CAN I HAVE MY PHONE IN MY BEDROOM?"

1. Adam Winsler et al., "Sleepless in Fairfax: The Difference One More Hour of Sleep Can Make for Teen Hopelessness, Suicidal Ideation, and Substance Use," *Journal of Youth and Adolescence* 44, no. 2 (Feb. 2015): 362–78.

2. American Academy of Pediatrics recommendations, in Victor C. Strasburger et al., "Sexuality, Contraception, and the Media," *Pediatrics* 126, no. 3 (Sept. 2010): 576–82, https://pediatrics.aappublications.org/content/126/3/576.full.

3. Megan A. Moreno, Yolanda Reid Chassiakos, and Corinn Cross, "Media Use in School-Aged Children and Adolescents," *Pediatrics* 138, no. 5 (Nov. 2016), https://pediatrics.aappublications.org/content/138/5/e20162592.

4. Michael B. Robb, *Screens and Sleep: The New Normal; Parents, Teens, Screens, and Sleep in the United States* (San Francisco, Common Sense Media, 2019), 26, https://www.commonsensemedia.org/sites/default/files/uploads/research/2019 -new-normal-parents-teens-screens-and-sleep-united-states-report.pdf.

5. Robb, *Screens and Sleep,* 25.

6. "Social Media, Social Life: Teens Reveal Their Experiences," Common Sense Media, September 10, 2018, https://www.commonsensemedia.org/social-media -social-life-infographic.

7. Jean Twenge, "Analysis: Teens Are Sleeping Less. Why? Smartphones," *PBS News Hour*, October 19, 2017, https://www.pbs.org/newshour/science/analysis-teens -are-sleeping-less-why-smartphones.

8. Jean M. Twenge, Zlatan Krizan, and Garrett Hisler, "Decreases in Self-Reported Sleep Duration among U.S. Adolescents 2009–2015 and Association with New Media Screen Time," *Sleep Medicine* 39 (Sept. 2017): 49, https://www. sciencedirect.com/science/article/abs/pii/S1389945717303507?via%3Dihub.

9. Robb, *Screens and Sleep,* 7.

10. Josh McDowell Ministry and Barna Group, *The Porn Phenomenon: The Explosive Growth of Pornography and How It's Impacting Your Church, Life, and Ministry* (Plano, TX: Josh McDowell Ministry, 2016), cited in Barna Group, "Porn in the Digital Age: New Research Reveals 10 Trends," April 6, 2016, http://barna.org /research/porn-in-the-digital-age-new-research-reveals-10-trends.

11. Markus Dworak et al., "Impact of Singular Excessive Computer Game and Television Exposure on Sleep Patterns and Memory Performance of School-aged Children," *Pediatrics* 120, no. 5 (Nov. 2007): 978–85, https://pediatrics .aappublications.org/content/120/5/978.short.

12. Robb, *Screens and Sleep,* 26.

13. Morning Consult, *The Influencer Report: Engaging Gen Z and Millennials,* cited in Sarah Min, "86% of Young Americans Want to Become a Social Media Influencer," CBS News, November 8, 2019, https://www.cbsnews.com/news/social-media -influencers-86-of-young-americans-want-to-become-one.

14. Robb, *Screens and Sleep,* 7.

15. Michelle D. Guerrero et al., "24-Hour Movement Behaviors and Impulsivity," *Pediatrics* 144, no. 3 (Sept. 2019), https://pediatrics.aappublications.org/content /144/3/e20190187.

16. "Improve Your Child's School Performance with a Good Night's Sleep," Sleep Foundation, accessed July 28, 2020, https://www.sleepfoundation.org/excessive -sleepiness/performance/improve-your-childs-school-performance-good-nights -sleep.

17. "Drowsy Driving Prevention, Teens Ages 16 to 19 Years," New York State Department of Health, revised February 2018, https://www.health.ny.gov /prevention/injury_prevention/children/fact_sheets/teens_15-19_years/drowsy _driving_16-19_years.htm.

18. Neeraj K. Gupta et al., "Is Obesity Associated with Poor Sleep Quality in Adolescents?" *American Journal of Human Biology* 14, no. 6 (Nov./Dec. 2002): 762–68, https://pubmed.ncbi.nlm.nih.gov/12400037/.

19. Robert E. Roberts and Hao T. Duong, "The Prospective Association between Sleep Deprivation and Depression among Adolescents," *Sleep* 37, no. 2 (Feb. 1, 2014): 239–44, https://www.ncbi.nlm.nih.gov/pmc/articles/PMC3900610/.

20. "Sleep and Mental Health: Sleep Deprivation Can Affect Your Mental Health," Harvard Mental Health Letter, Harvard Health Publishing, March 18, 2019, https://www.health.harvard.edu/newsletter_article/sleep-and-mental-health.

21. Winsler et al., "Sleepless in Fairfax," 370.

22. Judith Owens, Adolescent Sleep Working Group, and Committee on Adolescence, "Insufficient Sleep in Adolescents and Young Adults: An Update on Causes and Consequences," *Pediatrics* 134, no. 3 (Sept. 2014), https://pediatrics.aappublications .org/content/134/3/e921.

## CHAPTER 5: THE UNINTENDED EFFECTS OF SOCIAL MEDIA

1. 2017 National Survey on Drug Use and Health, cited in A. W. Geiger and Leslie Davis, "A Growing Number of American Teenagers—Particularly Girls—Are Facing Depression," Pew Research Center, July 12, 2019, https://www.pewresearch .org/fact-tank/2019/07/12/a-growing-number-of-american-teenagers-particularly -girls-are-facing-depression/.

2. Data from National Vital Statistics System (NVSS), cited in Sally C. Curtin and Melonie Heron, "Death Rates Due to Suicide and Homicide among Persons Aged 10–24: United States, 2000–2017," NCHS Data Brief, no. 352, October, 2019, https://www.cdc.gov/nchs/data/databriefs/db352-h.pdf.

3. Jean M. Twenge, "Stop Debating Whether Too Much Smartphone Time Can Hurt Teens, and Start Protecting Them," *Time*, March 21, 2019, https://time .com/5555737/smartphone-mental-health-teens/.

4. Jonathan Haidt and Jean Twenge, "Social Media Use and Mental Health: A Review" (unpublished manuscript, New York University, updated May 5, 2020),

https://docs.google.com/document/d/1w-HOfseF2wF9YIpXwUUtP65
-olnkPyWcgF5BiAtBEy0/edit.

5. Haidt and Twenge, "Social Media Use."

6. Haidt and Twenge, "Social Media Use."

7. Victoria Rideout and Michael B. Robb, *The Common Sense Census: Media Use by Teens and Tweens* (San Francisco: Common Sense Media, 2019), 12, table A, https://www.commonsensemedia.org/sites/default/files/uploads/research/2019 -census-8-to-18-full-report-updated.pdf.

8. Rideout and Robb, *Common Sense Census*, 11, table A.

9. Rideout and Robb, *Common Sense Census*, 13–14, table B.

10. Morning Consult, *The Influencer Report: Engaging Gen Z and Millennials*, cited in Sarah Min, "86% of Young Americans Want to Become a Social Media Influencer," CBS News, November 8, 2019, https://www.cbsnews.com/news/social-media -influencers-86-of-young-americans-want-to-become-one/.

11. Manisha Patel, "80% of Teenagers Want to Be Self-Employed in the Future and Are More Inclined to Be Freelancers," *Fintech Times*, May 30, 2020, https://thefintechtimes.com/80-of-teenagers-want-to-be-self-employed-in-the -future-and-are-more-inclined-to-be-freelancers/.

12. Jamie Ducharme, "A 12-Year-Old Girl Who Took Part in the 'Fire Challenge' Is in Intensive Care with Burns Covering Half Her Body," *Time*, August 23, 2018, https://time.com/5373180/fire-challenge/.

13. Rebecca Jennings, "Tikked Off: What Happens When TikTok Fame Fades," Vox, February 27, 2020, https://www.vox.com/the-goods/2020/2/27/21153364 /tiktok-famous-backlash.

14. Jason Ingram, Paul Brendon Mabury, and Lauren Daigle, "You Say," performed by Lauren Daigle, copyright 2018, Centricity.

## CHAPTER 6: THE THING ABOUT SCREEN TIME

1. Victoria Rideout and Michael B. Robb, *The Common Sense Census: Media Use by Teens and Tweens* (San Francisco: Common Sense Media, 2019), 3, https://www .commonsensemedia.org/sites/default/files/uploads/research/2019-census-8-to-18 -full-report-updated.pdf.

2. Rideout and Robb, *Common Sense Census*, 5.

3. Jenny Radesky and Dimitri Christakis, "Media and Young Minds," *Pediatrics* 138, no. 5 (Nov. 2016), https://pediatrics.aappublications.org/content/138/5/e20162591.

4. Radesky and Christakis, "Media and Young Minds."

5. Mayo Clinic Staff, "Screen Time and Children: How to Guide Your Child," Mayo Clinic, June 20, 2019, https://www.mayoclinic.org/healthy-lifestyle /childrens-health/in-depth/screen-time/art-20047952.

6. Radesky and Christakis, "Media and Young Minds."

7. Mayo Clinic Staff, "Screen Time and Children."

8. Chris Melore, "Sitting around Harmful to Teens' Mental Health; Just an Hour of

Light Activity Can Prevent Depression," Study Finds, May 25, 2020, https://www.studyfinds.org/sitting-around-harmful-to-teens-mental-health-just-an-hour-of-light-activity-can-prevent-depression/.

9. Melore, "Sitting around Harmful."

## CHAPTER 7: "I SEE YOU"

1. "Social Media, Social Life: Teens Reveal Their Experiences," Common Sense Media, September 10, 2018, https://www.commonsensemedia.org/social-media-social-life-infographic.

2. Survey conducted March 7–April 10, 2018, in Monica Anderson and Jingjing Jiang, *Teens, Social Media and Technology 2018* (Washington, DC: Pew Research Center, 2018), 2, https://www.pewresearch.org/internet/2018/05/31/teens-social-media-technology-2018/.

3. Ryan Broderick, "TikTok Has a Predator Problem. A Network of Young Women Is Fighting Back," BuzzFeed News, updated June 26, 2020, https://www.buzzfeednews.com/article/ryanhatesthis/tiktok-has-a-predator-problem-young-women-are-fighting-back.

4. Sheri Madigan et al., "Prevalence of Multiple Forms of Sexting Behavior among Youth: A Systematic Review and Meta-analysis," *JAMA Pediatrics* 172, no. 4 (2018): 327–35. doi:10.1001/jamapediatrics.2017.5314, https://jamanetwork.com/journals/jamapediatrics/fullarticle/2673719.

5. *Euphoria*, season 1, episode 1, "Pilot," directed by Augustine Frizzell, aired June 16, 2019, on HBO, quoted in Jonathan McKee, "What Parents Need to Know about Zendaya and Euphoria," *Jonathan's Blog*, August 6, 2019, https://jonathanmckeewrites.com/what-parents-need-to-know-about-zendaya-and-euphoria.

6. Janis Wolak, David Finkelhor, and Kimberly Mitchell, "Internet-Initiated Sex Crimes against Minors: Implications for Prevention Based on Findings from a National Study," *Journal of Adolescent Health* 35, no. 5 (2004): 11, http://unh.edu/ccrc/pdf/jvq/CV71.pdf.

7. Jonathan McKee and Alyssa McKee, *The Teen's Guide to Face-to-Face Connections in a Screen-to-Screen World* (Uhrichsville, OH: Shiloh Run Press, 2020), 148.

8. Russell Brandom, "New Bill Would Make Online Sexual Extortion a Federal Crime," *The Verge*, July 15, 2016, https://www.theverge.com/2016/7/15/12197712/sextortion-federal-crime-congress-katherine-clark.

9. Brandom, "New Bill." See also US Department of Justice, *The National Strategy for Child Exploitation Prevention and Interdiction: A Report to Congress—April 2016* (Washington, DC: Government Printing Office, 2016), 74–76, https://www.justice.gov/psc/file/842411/download.

10. US Department of Justice, *National Strategy*, 76.